MODERN BLACK LITERATURE

Chet Pryor
9005A Contee Rd.
Laurel, Md. 20708

SOMETHING OF LOVE by Franklyn Buell

Something of Love is a book of poems and essays about people, events and scenes from twenty-two years of newspaper reporting by the author in Massachusetts and New York. Moving cyclically through the seasons, the book holds to the bright side of life as the author looks back at subjects — the sunset, a good neighbor, and reminiscences of a boyhood on the Erie Canal.

Mr. Franklyn Buell, reporter for **Buffalo Evening News** since 1958 had worked on the staff of **The Springfield Union** for nearly ten years. Born in Connecticut in 1919, he lived as a boy in Georgia and served in World War II, including twenty months with the First Army Headquarters in Europe.

	150 pp. Cloth	$6.95 (Trade)
October 1971	LC Cat. No. 70-169534	ISBN 0-87831-025-8

MODERN BLACK LITERATURE
Edited by S. Okechukwu Mezu

Thirteen professors from three continents examine critical developments and trends in African, black American and West Indian poetry, drama and fiction, from black Renaissance to Negritude, from black autobiography to the folk and Calypso tradition in American and West Indian literature. Two chapters advance innovative ideas about darkening the curriculum through a comparative study of the literatures of expatriation and alienation. Originally a special issue of **Black Academy Review** (1971).

Dr. S. Okechukwu Mezu is editor of **Black Academy Review**, and Director of African Studies at the State University of New York at Buffalo.

LC Cat. No. 73-169535	Cloth $8.50	Paper $4.00
200 pp. Bibliography	ISBN 0-87831-020-7	0-87831-019-3

POLITICAL DEVELOPMENT AND SOCIAL CHANGE IN GHANA
A study of the influence of Kwame Nkrumah and the role of ideas in rapid social change.
by Francis A. Botchway

A comprehensive effort to analyze the impact of Nkrumah's ideas via the Convention People's Party on the development of Ghana. The study contains a mass of information and valuable data and deals both analytically and empirically with Nkrumah's attempt to institutionalize his ideas. Considerable new light is shed on Ghanaian social and political development in relation to Nkrumah and the CPP.

Dr. Francis A. Botchway, who is director of the Institute for Afro-American Studies at Richmond College, New York, has contributed a book of great value to students of African politics and to those professionals dealing with the problems of social change and political evolution.

	Eleven Tables	Bibliography
		160 pp.
October 1971	ISBN 0-87831-068-1	Cloth $8.00

BLACK ACADEMY PRESS, INC.
135 UNIVERSITY AVENUE, BUFFALO, NEW YORK 14214

MODERN BLACK LITERATURE

Edited by

Dr. S. Okechukwu Mezu

BLACK ACADEMY PRESS, INC.
BUFFALO, NEW YORK

*All rights reserved
including the right of reproduction
in whole or in part in any form*

Published by
BLACK ACADEMY PRESS, INC.
135 University Avenue
Buffalo, New York 14214
* * *
Box 104, Owerri, Nigeria
* * *
41 Leigham Vale, London, S.W. 16

Copyright © 1971 Black Academy Press, Inc.
ISBN 0-87831-019-3 Paper
ISBN 0-87831-020-7 Cloth
Library of Congress Catalog Card Number: 73-169535

Printed in the United States of America
Artcraft-Burow, Buffalo, New York

Contents

MODERN BLACK LITERATURE

BLACK RENAISSANCE AND NEGRITUDE	9	S. Okechukwu Mezu
THE POLITICS OF CONTEMPORARY AFRICAN LITERATURE	23	Jacob U. Gordon
PASSION AND POETRY IN THE WORKS OF DENNIS BRUTUS	41	Pol Ndu
ACHEBE'S "THINGS FALL APART"; AN IGBO NATIONAL EPIC	55	Charles E. Nnolim
BLACK AUTOBIOGRAPHY IN AFRICA AND AMERICA	61	Joseph Bruchac
BLACK AMERICAN POETRY: ITS LANGUAGE AND THE FOLK TRADITION	71	Alvin Aubert
RICHARD WRIGHT: THE EXPATRIATE PATTERN	81	Paul C. Sherr
"ANOTHER COUNTRY" AND THE SENSE OF SELF	91	Elliott M. Schrero
"DUTCHMAN" AND "THE SLAVE": COMPANIONS IN REVOLUTION	101	John Lindberg
CARIBBEAN LITERATURE IN ENGLISH: 1949-1970	109	R. M. Lacovia
THE CALYPSO TRADITION IN WEST INDIAN LITERATURE	127	Lloyd W. Brown
AN ASPECT OF AFRICAN AND CARIBBEAN THEATER IN FRENCH	145	Harold A. Waters
THE NEGRO THEATER IN BRAZIL	145	Abdias do Nascimento

A Special Issue of
Black Academy Review, Vol. 2, Nos. 1 & 2 (Spring-Summer), 1971

IGBO *Market Literature*

IGBO Market Literature, Veronica My Daughter, Forget Me Not, The Important Book for Nigerian Bachelors, The Gentle Giant Alakuku, What Is Life, Trust Nobody, Life is the Prison Yard, How To Start Life and End it Well, How To Marry a Good Girl, Light to Success, The Sweetness and Kingdom of Love, The Miracle of Love, Nancy in Blooming Youth, Beautiful Maria in the Art of True Love, They Died in the Game of Love.

Little John in the Love Adventure, Agnes in the Game of True Love, The Disappointed Lover, True Love, Born to be a Flirt, Queen of the Night, Disaster in the Realms of Love, One Love Forever, She Died in the Bloom of Youth, The Chains of Love, How to Speak to Girls and Win Their Love, The Lady Who Robbed Her Mother to Defend Her Husband, Stubborn Girl, Beware of Harlots and Many Friends, Between Love and Obedience, How to Make Friends With Girls.

Elizabeth My Lover, The Bitterness of Love, Right Way to Approach Ladies, Beauty Never Ends, Romance in a Nutshell, 9,000,000,000 Pound Man Still Says No Money, The Sorrows of Love, No Condition is Permanent, The World is Hard, Rose Only Loved My Money, Money Hard But Women Don't Know, the Last Days of Lumumba, Dr. Nkrumah in the Struggle for Freedom, The Struggles and Trials of Jomo Kenyatta, The Statements of Hitler, The Life Story of Zik, The Life and Death of JFK, How Tshombe and Mobutu . . .

IGBO MARKET LITERATURE
Edited by S. Okechukwu Mezu

The classics of the Onitsha Market in Nigeria. Unique phenomenon in Africa. More than 4,000 original pages, unexpurgated, unabashed, ungrammatical, earthy, vibrant, hilarious, incredible often, but definitely healthy and revealing of the **real** Africa for the young and the adult.

Sometimes called the Onitsha Chap books, they are the veritable cradles of modern African literature, and possibly the only **authentic** black African literature in modern times written by the people for the people. No serious study of modern African literature and culture can be done without reference to these unique documents uninfluenced by cartesian logic, unpolluted by Western erudition and unhaunted by the desire to cater to a foreign market.

For the first time ever the chap books are presented together after years of search and research in five convenient volumes — a collector's item. Sold only as a set.

IGBO MARKET LITERATURE
5 Volumes. Illustrations. $100.00
(Orders before July 30, 1971 — $80.00)
ISBN 0-87831-060   L.C.C.C. No. 77-169536
BLACK ACADEMY PRESS, INC.
135 UNIVERSITY AVENUE, BUFFALO, NEW YORK 14214

INDIANA UNIVERSITY is seeking a CHAIRMAN for its PROGRAM IN AFRO-AMERICAN STUDIES. Suggested criteria for the position: demonstrated commitment to Afro-American Studies; willingness to work closely with black students; preferably under 35, with doctorate in appropriate field; administrative experience or interest; publications in Afro-American Studies, in print and in progress.

Send vita: Herman Hudson, Vice Chancellor
Afro-American Affairs, Indiana University
Bloomington, Indiana 47401

NOW AVAILABLE IN SPECIAL LIBRARY BINDING (Gold on Blue)
BLACK ACADEMY REVIEW, VOL. 1, 1970
Quarterly of the black world.
Including the Index. Cloth $12.00

BLACK ACADEMY REVIEW, INC.
135 University Avenue, Buffalo, N. Y. 14214

SPECIAL PROGRAMS IN AMERICAN UNIVERSITIES
A look at the myriads of special programs at American schools from Head Start and Upward Bound to Black and Puerto-Rican Studies Programs as well as participant attitudes to such programs on predominantly white campuses.
ISBN 0-87831-013-4   Cloth $5.00   82 pp.

BLACK ACADEMY PRESS, INC.
135 University Avenue, Buffalo, N. Y. 14214

BLACK RENAISSANCE AND NEGRITUDE
By
S. Okechukwu Mezu

On October 21, 1850, Sainte-Beuve set out to define classicism with a great deal of hesitation. "A delicate question," he said, "and one to which according to the time and age, one could very well propose rather diverse solutions. Someone asked me the question today, and I would like to try if not to solve it, at least to examine it, to explore it in front of the readers, even if only to engage in a search for a solution and if I can, to make clearer your and my conception of the subject." Sainte-Beuve went on to say that classicism meant a different thing for the Romans, and for the modernists during the reign of Louis XIV or even when the word classicism was defined with respect to Romanticism. Sainte-Beuve finally concluded that every epoch, every reader, will very likely maintain his own definition of classicism. This is very true of negritude.

Montaigne in his essay, "De l'Expérience" said also that "no two men have ever judged in the same way the same thing, and it is impossible to see two opinions exactly similar, not only in different people, but in the same man at divers times". Critics are essentially human and are likely to judge issues differently. Negritude means something different to every one and each writer or critic sees in the word what is of interest to him. The marxist looks at it in economic terms, in terms of conflict and class struggle. Thus the marxist equates various aspects of the negritude movement as revolutionary or conservative.

Jean-Paul Sartre in his article "Orphée noir" sees the movement as a struggle to overthrow the oppressive forces of cultural domination, a struggle similar to the proletarian effort to dethrone the capitalist structure by replacing it with the dictatorship of the proletariat or a classless society. But whereas the proletarian revolt is economic and physical, the negritude revolt is intellectual and humanistic since the values at stake are not economic and material but cultural and aesthetic. The negritude effort therefore is to implant a "dictatorship" of black cultural values that will naturally lead to a non-race-conscious society.

The anthropologists, on the other hand, especially the essentialists amongst them, see the negritude movement basically as a cultural assertion and manifestation of the old Africa in the modern world. An attempt is made to find, and often when they do not quite exist, to create a sort of life force that supposedly governs the actions and reactions of the black man. The anthropologist sharing this view then equates negritude as the black or the African way of writing, the African or black world view, *Weltanschauung, vision du monde*. Any black writer that does not quite fit into the general pattern established by the essentialist is considered one who has abandoned the basic and all-embracing philosophy of his people.

For some sociologists, negritude is basically the result of the intermingling of the social forces of the century. It is a result of the conflict between the old and the new, the effort to conserve and modernize, the struggle between races, the color problem which William Du Bois at the beginning of the century said would be the major problem facing the generations to come.

Negritude is thus seen as the sudden sometimes shocking realization by the black man that he is black and that his color is no longer accidental but substantial and consequential, and perhaps fatal. Negritude thus becomes a type of literary ghetto in the Western world, as revealing, depriving and exploited as the urban ghettoes of contemporary cities. Some psychologists see negritude as some kind of sublimation, an outpouring of centuries of repressed feelings simmering in the collective unconscious, feelings that have finally found expression in a unique kind of way in literary creation. Persecution complex, transference, the other, usually the white man, form the solid or rather shaky basis for this literature. Such a view would make the literature of negritude a therapeutic process favouring greatly the creation of poetry and the writing of autobiographical novels. The individual psychoanalyses himself in order to save himself from madness. The writer lays the blame on the other, the oppressor, the white man, in order to justify the status of his people if not his own.

But there is also the traditional critic who sees negritude as a literary phenomenon, a humanism that symbolizes an epoch, that describes an era and characterizes a certain generation. Negritude, the traditional critic contends, should rightfully take its place at least in African, if not in black and world literary history, just like its great antecedents in the western culture, movements like the Renaissance, Classicism, Romanticism, Symbolism and Surrealism.

There is certainly an element of truth in these various definitions of the idea, the notion, the concept, the movement of negritude, for it is all of these things.

But each definition, each view, each approach, in wishing to be exclusive does injustice to the whole idea and tells only a partial truth. It was Aristotle who wrote in Tome I, Book II of his *Metaphysics* that no one can grasp adequately the truth, or even miss it completely. Each philosopher, he continued, finds something to say about nature. In itself, this contribution is nothing without doubt, or of little importance, but the totality of the ideas and reflections produces fruitful results. To add to this, from a purely structural point of view, man is indivisible and cannot realistically be divorced from his society, the collective unconscious, traditions and progress, aspirations and realizations. The African or black writer of the negritude period is therefore both an individual and a product of his society, a cousin of the modern world of technological superinventions and a child of the traditional world of cosmic animim. He is both a product of colonialism and slavery as well as the independence movement and the struggle for equal rights; a victim of western prejudice and an heir of western enlightenment. He is in short the product of opposing forces, the unism of traditional African life and the dualism of centuries of western civilization. A fair examination of the meaning of negritude therefore should take into consideration all these varied and sometimes opposing forces and feelings—historical, sociological, economic, political and even psycho-somatic forces that try to shape and unshape individuals and nations. A brief literary history would perhaps best situate negritude in a structural world.

For centuries, for more than three thousand years, the white writer, writing for a white audience has written from a white point of view. Dante, Petrarch, Ronsard, Schiller, Lamartine, Eluard, Hugo, Spencer, Yeats, have been singing the beauty of the white world, in particular the white woman, her blond hair, her blue eyes, her white fingers, red lips and rosy cheeks that blush at the sight of the loved one. The white writer has praised and glorified this beauty because it is an integral part of his experience, his white experience. The black woman rarely appeared in this literature. When as in the case of Jeanne Duval, she plays an important role in the life of a poet Baudelaire, she is a prostitute and her beauty is always considered satanic, her inspiration devlish, her affection, the antipode of real love. A white angelic beauty like Madame Sabatier, lofty, inaccessible, "pure", is set up in contrast to her. And even with Jeanne Duval, Baudelaire's attention is not on the woman as an individual. The prostitute is merely utilized as an instrument of escape to the tropics. What counts is not the beauty of her long hair but the associations it conjours and the evocations it recalls. Sometimes also in the letters of Le Chevalier de Boufflers to Madame la Comtesse de Sabran between 1778-1788, mostly written from Senegal, a young black girl appears on the European scene in a Parisian home but always as an ethnic curiosity. Generally, the treatment of blacks in Western Literature has left much to be desired. Sometimes it is in the form of biting irony, at other times caustic sarcasm and elsewhere barefaced racism. These are everywhere and are often found in the most unlikely places, including Cervantes' *Don Quixote*, Montesquieu's *Esprit des Lois*, in Benjamin Franklin, Hegel, Rimbaud's "Mauvais Sang" in *Une saison en enfer* and in William Blake's "The Little Black Boy", in *Songs of Innocence* in which the poet writes:

> My mother bore me in the southern wild,
> And I am black, but O! my soul is white;
> White as an angel is the English child,
> But I am black, as if bereav'd of light.

Later the prejudice against the black man would become more pronounced and articulate with writers like Arthur de Gobineau in his *Essai sur l'inégalité des races humaines* (1854) and with Gustave Le Bon in his *Lois psychologiques de l'évolution des peuples*.

Whites for a long time did all the writing that was done and most of the reading too. Coupled with all these, whites created quite a few things and discovered many more including the dark continent of Africa, "dark" in color and intelligence. Whites set up various scales based upon their own experiences. One of these scales is the solar hierarchy within which, arbitrarily, white was a symbol of glory and joy while black became synonymous with sorrow and mourning. Whiteness became associated with the beauty of the day and darkness with sorrows and hallucinations of the night. The useless member of a group became also the *black-sheep of the family*. Even Arthur Rimbaud in his colored audition unconsciously underscored this phenomenon in his assignment of properties to white and black:

(A: Noir)
A, Noir corset velu des mouches éclatantes
Qui bombinent autour des puanteurs cruelles,
Golfes d'ombres

(E: Blanc)
E, candeurs des vapeurs et des tentes
Lances des glaciers fiers, rois blancs, frissons d'ombelles.

In addition to all the other disadvantages, there was also the slave trade which snatched from Africa over four hundred million blacks and put them in plantations in the Americas and the West Indies. Not satisfied perhaps with these indignities, the whites came also to Africa to colonize and exploit the area and fourteen small European "nations" divided amongst themselves in Berlin in 1886 the gigantic continent, the "tribes" of Africa that had escaped the mass enslavement of their people. Just as in America, the slave owners made no effort to understand the feelings of their slaves, their customs and their attitude to life and used them just as animals of burden, the men for their economic welfare, the women for their sexual gratification, so too in Africa, the French amongst other people around 1906 introduced the policy of assimilation which sought to make every black African within their sphere of influence a little white Frenchman, beginning with courses on the history of their "ancestors, the Gauls of Roman times". The British for their part, generally left the people alone as long as they did not revolt against their rule. But sometimes they created chiefs where there were none, amongst the Igbos for instance; and deposed them where they had centuries of customs, history and royalty behind them, the Obas of Lagos for instance. The course of history and literature was fine as long as there was no challenge to this white view of the world. *Blanchitude* reigned supreme because there was no *negritude* to challenge it. The white audience was not aware of this or purposely closed its eyes to it because light becomes light only in the presence of darkness. A crisis, an existentialist crisis was necessary to shock the world into the conscious realization of the black presence.

THE BLACK RENAISSANCE

This black presence became felt at the middle of the nineteenth century. One can really speak of a *Black Renaissance* in literature and the arts. The 1848 abolition of the slave trade gave moment to this movement and that date can be considered a landmark in the black Renaissance movement as 1453 was to the European Renaissance of the 16th century. Before then, the Negro's conception of self was always based on comparison with the white man. In the words of William Du Bois in *Souls of Black Folk*

> After the Egyptian and Indian, the Greek and Roman, the Teuton and Mongolian, the Negro is a sort of seventh son, born with a veil, and gifted with second-sight in this American world—a world which yields him no true self-consciousness but only lets him see himself through the revelation of the other world. It is a peculiar sensation, this double-consciousness, this sense of always looking at one's self through the eyes of others, of measuring one's soul by the tape of a world that looks on in amused contempt and pity."
> (Souls of Black Folk, *Three Negro Classics*, pp. 214-215)

Booker T. Washington, writing about the Reconstruction period in America, emphasized the importance of Latin at the beginning of the period. Two ideas were constantly agitating the minds of the colored people, or at least the minds of a large part of the race. One of them, he says was the craze for Greek and Latin learning, and the other was a desire to hold office. Then, he continues, there was a feeling that a knowledge, however little, of the Greek and Latin languages would make one a very superior human being, something bordering almost on the supernatural. This search for Greek antiquity will sooner or later give rise to another search equally vital and more pertinent and relevant, the quest for their own historical sources, the quest for Africa and black values, the height of which will come at the turn of the century.

In 1897, for example, Alexander Crummel organized the Washington Negro-American Academy, a movement of defense to rally black intellectuals of America for the sake of promoting research on problems affecting the black man. In 1900, a lawyer from Trinidad, H. Sylvester Williams, with the support of Bishop Alexander Walters of the African Methodist Episcopal Zion Church, a black separatist church, organized the first Pan-African Congress. In the United States of America, following a manifesto launched in 1905 by William Du Bois, the Niagara Falls conference was called and after further reunions gave rise to the National Association for the Advancement of Colored People (N.A.A.C.P.) in 1910. Through its Journal, *The Crisis* (1909), this organization was able to influence and spur on cultural awakening of the black man in United States. The black man was awakening from a prolonged sleep. He was looking for a way of coming out of his shell, of getting rid of his lethargy. More con-

BLACK RENAISSANCE AND NEGRITUDE 15

scious of his individuality, he wanted to liberate himself and once free to liberate his brethren. The black man was no longer ready to accept as a dogma all that is brought to him by religion or history. He was no longer satisfied with being a *slave* or even an *emancipated slave* in America and a *native* or even an *educated native* in Africa. He was no longer ready to submit himself to western values abroad and suffer colonial domination on the motherland. And colonial domination there was for by 1902, the map of the black continent showed an Africa divided among the so-called European powers: England, France, Germany, Portugal, Belgium, Italy, Turkey, Spain. Only Morocco, Ethiopia and Liberia were independent. As if to emphasize its decision to stay forever in Africa, for administrative and economic reasons, France was creating federations in Africa. The French West African Federation in 1904 and the French Equatorial African Federation in 1910. England followed in 1914 with the creation of the Federation of Nigeria, the *Amalgamation* of the Northern, and Southern Protectorates and the Colony of Lagos.

On the other hand, the black man, the African in Africa, his descendants in the new world, were in direct contact with the white man. Africans undertook voyages of discovery and at the turn of the century, the black intellectual will discover unexplored lands, the unexplored new lands of Europe and America, the slave jungles of America that brutalized and cannibalized millions of their relations, the native belligerence and barbarism of the white European that would be reconfirmed in 1914. Having discovered these new worlds, the African will never cease to explore these territories, to study them, analyze them, and unmask them. A new horizon was spreading before the world. It is in this context that one should examine the writings of Wilmot Blyden, William Du Bois, some aspects of the teachings of Booker T. Washington and the politics of Marcus Garvey with his "Back to Africa" movement, which sought to repatriate blacks to the African continent. Blacks intensified their formation, at this period, of black separatist churches as a protest against segregation in the white dominated protestant churches. These cultural, political and religious agitations of various kinds manifested a new sentiment.

Though separated from it by four centuries, this movement can be compared to the European Renaissance, especially the French one, of the sixteenth century, the *white Renaissance.* That renaissance marked a break with the Middle Ages, the *Dark Ages,* the mode of thinking, accepted ideas. It marked a new consciousness on the part of the white humanist who discovered that his white patrimony went back to Greco-Roman times. This discovery of the self on the part of the European did not come suddenly but due to a long transition and as a result of disparate movements and more particularly to the flight of artists towards the West following the capture in 1453 by the Turks of Constantinople. The idea here is not to set up in this twentieth century an analogy of events in Europe in the 16th century but the similarity is nevertheless real. For the black man of the twentieth century, the 1848 abolition of slavery can be considered as the major incident that unleashed the movement.

Though emancipation in the United States came later, it is recognized that 1848 signalled a new age of greater militancy and radicalism in the abolitionist movement with Frederick Douglas, up till then basically a moderate and an advocate of moral suasion, increasingly adopting the philosophies of the militant John Brown and the fiery Henry Garnet who exhorted his people in these terms:

> Brethren, arise, arise! Strike for your lives and liberties. Now is the day and the hour. Let every slave throughout the land do this, and the days of slavery are numbered. You cannot be more oppressed than you have been; you cannot suffer greater cruelties than you have already. *Rather die freemen than live to be slaves.*

Just as the geographical discoveries of the European Renaissance enlarged the horizons and supposedly the minds of the Europeans, the voyages for study and research, for campaigns and diplomacy of Africans and black Americans in Europe, of black West Indians in America, Europe and Africa, revealed a new world to them. These future humanists will illuminate the way for future black scholars, writers and artists. What Benjamin Banneker tried to do with science, Wilmot Blyden battled to demonstrate with his humanism. Wilmot Blyden, of *pure Negro descent from the Igbo tribe* (like Olauda Ekweano, better known as Gustavus Vassa, author of *The Interesting Narrative of the Life of Olaudah Equiano or Gustavus Vassa the African, Written by Himself—1789*), wrote *A Vindication of the African Race: being a brief examination of the argument in favour of African Inferiority* (1857) and *The Negro in Ancient History* (1869).

The two Renaissance movements encouraged a critical approach to life and brought about a certain kind of rupture with the past. New modes of worship were opened as man sought to free himself from the strong arms of decadent tradition. As the

African Methodist and Episcopal churches multiplied in America, and as the English in Africa continued to use christianity to destroy cherished African traditions, Wilmot Blyden advocated the establishment of Africa-based churches.

In fact the United Native African Church was formed in 1891. A new liberal humanism was bringing down the rigid walls of traditional erudition. In the European Renaissance, more important than the awakening consciousness on the part of the individual, the race and the nation; more important than the rupture with the ancient political and religious order was a new humanism, a new quest for pagan antiquity. This quest in Europe of the sixteenth century gave rise to new scholarship and in turn influenced the literary style as well as styles in painting and sculpture. At the turn of the century, the black man also wanted, during his Renaissance, to glorify his past, his "pagan" antiquity, the past for long lost and only recently rediscovered due to the tireless efforts of black humanists. There was a new sense of being, a new optimism developing. The black man at the beginning of the century recognized that Africa was not a continent without culture and civilization but on the contrary, the source of cultures, the living museum of ancient civilizations. Africa was not a *tabula rasa*. Black humanists had spoken and spoke about the contributions of Africa to civilization: Tertulian, Augustine of Hippo, J. Africanus Horton and Wilmot Blyden spoke about Africa's contributions to Egyptian and Greek civilizations. The kingdoms of Ghana, Songhai, Biafra, Bini, Mali as well as the universities of Timbucktu and the art centers of Ife and Ugbo-Ukwu would be resurrected.

As the European Renaissance gave rise to new forms of art and music, the Black Renaissance and the discovery of African art would give rise to the Cubist Movement in painting. As early as 1907 Pablo Picasso in his *Femme* (sketch for *Les Demoiselles d'Avignon*) and in the same year the masterpiece itself, *Les Demoiselles d'Avignon*, was opening a new era in modern painting. African influence is evident in his *Figure* (Paris 1907) and *Figurine* (Paris 1908) the latter in bronze. In his painting and in his sculpture, just as in traditional African art, Picasso tried to destroy the physical form in order to capture and suggest the essential quality of the subject, which exists not in time and space but in the immateriality of life. In music also, the beginning of the century marked the ascendency of jazz and blues and in Paris of *la béguine* a West Indian dance popularized by Josephine Baker.

European white scholars stepped into the show also as Leo Frobenius, Maurice Delafosse, Henri Labouret, (in Africa) Ferdinand Ortiz in Cuba began their ethnological or anthropological studies of the black races, sympathetic, though still from the European optique. William Du Bois contributed also his history book *The Negro* (1915) as *The Association for the Study of Negro Life and History* was formed in Washington, D.C. African civilization became an interesting field of study and political and missionary volunteers were everywhere. Even Albert Schweitzer, representing *Dives* (Luke 16: 19-31), the white man endowed with all the benefits of "culture and science", left in 1913 for Gabon in Africa to help *Lazarus,* representing the Negro, exploited and oppressed and lacking even "European" medicine for his disease and pain, the consequences of his oppression. African artifacts graced Parisian and London living rooms and several special editions of magazines were consecrated to Africa. Journalists vulgarized the discoveries or the writings of the anthropologists. In America, *The Crisis* played a leading role in the cultural awakening of the new world. On its staff then were Dr. Du Bois, James Weldon Johnson, Walter White and Jessie Fauset.

The culmination of these movements, in literature at least, was the Harlem Renaissance in New York and over in Europe the Negritude Movement in Paris. The Harlem Renaissance, a period in the greater movement of Black Renaissance, unleashed a black, vibrant and creative energy. Inspired by black humanists, black writers emerged and successfully challenged the system imposed by white writers on the literary world. The year 1925 can be considered the summit of the movement in Harlem. Alain Locke was certainly one of its most articulate exponents, at least from the theoretical point of view. Describing this phenomenon, in "The New Negro", in *The New Negro: An Interpretation* (1925), he writes:

> In the last decade something beyond the watch and guard of statistics has happened in the life of the American Negro and the three norms who have traditionally presided over the Negro problem have a changeling in their laps. The Sociologist, the Philanthropist, the Race-leader are not unaware of the New Negro, but they are at a loss to account for him. He simply cannot be swathed in their formulae. For the younger generation is vibrant with a new psychology; the new spirit is awake in the masses, and in the very eyes of the professional observers is transforming what has been a perennial problem into the progressive phases of contemporary Negro life.

Alain Locke spoke of the migrant masses shifting from the countryside to the city, hurdling several generations of experience at a leap. He spoke about the changing life-attitudes and self-expression of the young Negro, in his poetry, his art, his education and his new outlook, full of poise and greater knowledge of what it is all about. What Alain Locke articulated philosophically, Claude McKay described in his novel, *Banjo*, a marvellous apologetics of black culture.

A whole new vocabulary was introduced into the field of literature. Certainly, had Phyllis Wheatley lived during the period of the Black Renaissance, her poetry would have been radically different. James Weldon Johnson in "O Black and Unknown Bards" wrote:

> O black and unknown bards of long ago,
>   How came your lips to touch the sacred fire?
> How, in your darkness, did you come to know
>   The power and beauty of the minstrel's lyre?
> Who first from midst his bonds lifted his eyes?
>   Who first from out the still watch, lone and long,
> Feeling the ancient faith of prophets rise
>   Within his dark-kept soul, burst into song?

There is no revolution, as of yet, from the point of view of syntax and versification but in that poem already a new set of vocabulary is introduced into the literary world. *Black, Darkness,* and similar words suddenly lose their traditional connotation in white literature.

In *God's Trombones: some Negro sermons in verse,* James Weldon Johnson will also introduce the Negro rhythm into literature. Describing a Negro preacher, James Johnson said:

> An electric current ran through the crowd. It was in a moment alive and quivering; and all the while the preacher held it in the palm of his hand. He was wonderful in the way he employed his conscious and unconscious art. He strode the pulpit up and down in what was actually a very rhythmic dance, and he brought into play the full gamut of his wonderful voice, a voice—what shall I say —not of an organ or a trumpet, but rather of a trombone; the instrument possessing above all others the power to express the wide and varied range of emotions encompassed by the human voice—and with greater amplitude. He intoned, he moaned, he pleaded—he blared, he crashed, he thundered. I sat fascinated; any more, I was, perhaps against my will, deeply moved; the emotional effect upon me was irresistible.

This is a combination of poetry, prose, song and music in the typical African fashion. The music is not only external but internal, conscious and subconscious. The sufferings of the race are depicted, the aspirations of the people are suggested. In a poetic trance, the preacher, like the *griot* of Senegal, the *onye-ntu* of Igboland, abandons himself, his whole being as a medium to the inspiration from within, from above, as he sings, chants, forecasts, foretells, admonishes, praises and castigates to prick the conscience of the wicked, encourage the suffering and the dying— and also to the fright of children awakened by his or her voice (pleading, intoning, crashing, shrilling, thundering, blaring, supplicating, moaning, fascinating, emotional, firm, irresistible, fading, dying . . . .) in the middle of the night.

Writers, then in America, who hesitated about the new movement were greatly encouraged by *The Souls of Black Folk* (1903) of William Du Bois, printed and reprinted over and over. William S. Braithewaite spoke for quite a few members of the race when in Locke's anthology, *The New Negro*, he wrote that *The Souls of Black Folk* "has more profoundly influenced the spiritual temper of the race than any other written in its generation."

The revolution in vocabulary continued. Countée Cullen in his "Tableau" would refer to the color black as "the sable pride of night" and Claude McKay would in "The Tropics in New York" tantalize the temperate and white world with the luscious freshness of tropical fruits:

> Bananas ripe and green, and ginger root,
>   Cocoa in pods and alligator pears,
> And tangerines and mangoes and grape fruit,
>   Fit for the highest prize at parish fairs.

In Jean Toomer's *Cane*, the color black loses also its derogatory connotations for Negro slaves are referred to as "dark purple ripened plums, squeezed, and bursting in the pine-wood air . . ." The River Seine, The Rhine and the Rhone will no longer dominate the literature of the future for there is a Langston Hughes to Speak of Rivers, the Nile, the Congo "ancient as the world and older than the flow of human blood in human veins". The Negro was no longer ashamed of his color. He was even ready to exhibit its beauty as Langston Hughes in "Jazzonia" published in *The Crisis*:

> What jungle tree have you slept under,
>   Midnight dancer of the jazzy hour?
> What great forest has hung its perfume
>   Like a sweet veil about your bower?
>
> What jungle tree have you slept under,
>   Dark-brown girl of the swaying hips?
> What star-white moon has been your lover?
>   To what mad faun have you offered your lips?

With Countée Cullen's "Heritage," the Negro will learn to speak with pride. The Sun will have the color of copper and black will become the symbol of royalty. The real revolution had been achieved in American literature, it would be up to the future generation to push this revolt to the point of anarchy, the total destruction of the white man's language, syntax and idioms, a total negation of white values and structures, a point achieved some thirty years later in the sixties, a polarization that will no doubt give rise to a synthesis of ideas, structures and styles.

Hopefully, words would recover their denotations or syntactical representations as blacks continue to push their racial pride to its logical conclusion and as whites begin to realize that there are other than white perspectives on life.

The wind of the American revolt, the Harlem Renaissance in Literature, was blowing all around Europe where a gradual re-examination of African civilization had already begun with the help of French and European writers, scholars and artists. Langston Hughes, William Du Bois and Claude McKay made several trips to Europe where they met blacks from Africa and the West Indies—Blaise Diagne, Dr. Leo Sajous, Paulette Nardal, Jean Price-Mars. Leo Sajous and Paulette through their review *La Revue du monde noir*, between November 1931 and April 1932, popularized the Harlem Renaissance through articles on black literature and civilization. One of their aims was to "create among the Blacks of the entire world, without distinction of nationality, a moral and an intellectual bond that will allow them to better love and understand one another fraternally, to defend more efficaciously their collective interests and to embellish their Race". The editors of the new publication were well aware of the movement in New York. They even knew about the Harlem review *Fire* (only one issue was ever published) edited by a Pleiade of Harlem writers—Wallace Thurman, Aaron Douglas, John P. Davis, Bruce Nugent, Gwendolyn Bennet, Zora Neale Hurston and Langston Hughes. In their Paris publication, they reproduced the words of Langston Hughes in the introduction:

> We younger Negro artists who create now intend to express our individual darkskinned selves without fear or shame. If white people are pleased, we are glad. If they are not, it doesn't matter . . . If colored people are pleased, we are glad. If they are not, their displeasure doesn't matter either.

At the same time in Paris were three young students, among many others, Leopold Senghor from Senegal, Aimé Césaire from the Martinique and Léon Damas from the Guadeloupe. They could not escape the ferment created by the interest in black civilization. They read every word published in *La Revue du monde noir* and held long discussions with the elder generation at the home of Paulette Nardal. Imbued with a new sense of mission, without a formal decision they set out to accomplish for the French-speaking black world what the Harlem writers had done for the English-speaking world.

Personal experience of racism in Europe reinforced their racial pride. The failure of European science and technology as well as its rationalism confirmed their newly-found belief that black civilization alone held the answer to man's future. These antiracist feelings were redoubled by the growing racism in Germany, fascism in Italy and Spain and the struggle against the Machado regime in Cuba. In the midst of these developments, disturbed by the failure of white wisdom to prevent the First World War and its consequent disruption of society, the white writers themselves were turning to Surrealism for social and cultural salvation. The young students in Paris, Senghor in particular, saw in the surrealist technique an imitation of the black African traditional poet. The Surrealist was out to bridge the gap between dreams and reality, science and fiction, the material and the spiritual world. They delved into their unconscious, after Freud had revealed it to them, to discover this world. The Senegalese Senghor could look down on them with scorn because, he argued, in Africa, man had not yet been divorced from his ancestors and his environment. When *La Revue du monde noir* ceased publication, another review came up, *Légitime Défense* edited by Etienne Lero and his group of friends, with a socialist and marxist orientation. Senghor, Cesaire and Damas with their friends organized their own magazine (1934/35) *L'Etudiant noir*. Like the Harlem *Fire* only one issue came to light. There, like their Harlem counterparts, they sought to articulate their blackness irrespective of the reaction of white people and black people alike.

These and a combination of other forces gave rise to the literature of negritude. Any attempt to define the word *Negritude* must therefore take into consideration its origins and its place within the context of the development of the black civilization during the Black Renaissance.

THE POLITICS OF CONTEMPORARY AFRICAN LITERATURE

by

Jacob U. Gordon

Literature has been described as the expression of the experiences of a people. It provides, as such, a vivid reflection of the joys, sorrows, aspirations and dreams of the group. There is, therefore, no better place to seek the reaction of Africans to their situations and to learn their thoughts than in the works of their writers.

What have been the experiences of Africans as colonized peoples? What are their reactions to these experiences and how have they manifested these reactions? Any study of African literature must take into consideration the observed facts and events of the African's life and his recounting of them. Such an undertaking must consider the confrontation of African culture with that of the West and the African's determination to maintain his essential dignity as a man and to assert his own personality.

This paper deals mainly with contemporary literature with little reference to the wealth of oral literature (tales, songs, proverbs) which is the prime repository for the wit and wisdom of the people. This tribal lore is often the source of contemporary tales, novels, poems, and dramas.

Writers from the former French territories, in West and Equatorial Africa, former British territories of West and East Africa and South Africa, are included. Colonial policy, which had a significant effect upon the literature, was different in each of these regions. This is not to say that one finds homogeneity of thought or expression among writers of any particular region. The variety of ethnic groupings, "tribes and clans" with their different languages, social systems, customs and conventions of religions, practice of art — the sum total of activities which members of a group share in common — identify them from other groups no matter how closely related. Thus the poet Abioseh Nicol of Sierra Leone, a scientist and university professor gives a clear view of the situation in his poem, "The Meaning of Africa":

> You are not a country, Africa,
> You are a concept,
> Fashioned in our minds, each to each,
> To hide our separate fears,
> To dream our separate dreams . . .

One of the greatest influences on contemporary Africa was the invasion of their continent by the Europeans. How do Africans feel about colonialism? What are their reactions to the taking of their land by outside forces which subjected them to indignities and relegated them to places of inferior importance in their own lands? One of the frequent attacks found in African literature is the one against "Civilization" since "to civilize the savages" was the pretext used by the colonizers to justify their invasion of the so-called Dark Continent. As early as 1921, Rene Maran said in the Preface of *Batouala* "Civilization, Civilization, pride of Europeans and their slaughter house of innocents, Rabindranath Tagore, the Hindu poet, once in Tokyo, told what you are: You build your kingdom on corpses. Whatever you wish, whatever you do, is steeped in lies . . . You are not a torch, but a fire. Whatever you touch, you devour." *Batouala,* the first important French African novel is as scathing and effective a condemnation of colonialism as can be found anywhere. Most African poets agree with Maran, in his attack on colonialism.

Leopold Senghor says in his first volume of poetry *Chants d'ombre:* "They cut down the forests of Africa to save civilization for there was a shortage of human raw-material." In 1922 a Senegalese student, Amadou Moustapha Wade, wrote in a poem published in *Les Etudiants noirs parlent:*

> But here come the "Civilizers"
> With cannon and Bible aimed
> at the African's heart.

Later a Cameroonian poet wrote a poem entitled "Civilization" (translated here from the French):

> They found me in the healthy shade
> of my bamboo hut
> they found me
> dressed in *obom* and animal skins

with my palavers
and my torrential laughter
with my tom toms
my gris-gris
and my gods

What a pity! How primitive he is!
Let's civilize him.
Then they showered my head
with their wordy books
then they bedecked my body
with their own gris-gris
then they inoculated me
in my blood
my bright transparent blood
with avarice
and alcoholism
and prostitution
and incest
and fratricidal politics

Hurrah!
Behold me now, a civilized man.

The suffering of the Blacks under the rule of the Colonialist is a favorite theme with writers. David Diop, a young poet born in France of Sengalese parents, presents a bitter protest in "Souffre, pauvre Negre." The poem ends:

The lash stings
stings — your back of sweat and blood
Suffer, poor Negro
The day is long —
So long — as you carry the white ivory of your master the white
    man.
Your children are hungry
Hungry and your hut is empty —
Empty of your wife who is sleeping —
who is sleeping in the master's bed.
suffer, poor Negro.
Negro black as grief.

Senghor in his "Prayer for Peace," dedicated to his former classmate Georges Pompidou and Mme. Pompidou asks God to forgive white Europe for the sins it has committed against Africa.

Lord God, forgive white Europe.
It is true Lord, that for four enlightened centuries,
    she has scattered the baying and slaver of her mastiffs
    over my lands

and the Christians forsaking Thy light and the gentleness of Thy heart
Have lit their camp fires with my parchments, tortured my disciples deported my doctors and masters of science
Their powder has crumbled in a flash the pride of tatas and hills
And their bullets have gone through the bowels of vast empires like daylight, from the Horn of the West to the Eastern Horizon.
They have fired the intangible woods like hunting grounds, dragged out
Ancestors and spirits by their peaceable beards, and turned their mystery into Sunday distraction for somnamulant bourgeois.
Lord forgive them who turned the Askia into "Maquisards," my princes into sergeant-majors, my household servants into "boys", my peasants into wage-earners, my people into a working class.
For Thou must forgive those who have hunted my children like wild elephants.
And broken them in with whips, have made them the black hands of those whose hands were white.
For Thou must forget those who exported ten millions of my sons in the leperhouses of their ships.
Who killed two hundred millions of them.
And have made for me a solitary old age in the forest of my nights and the savannah of my days.
Lord, the glasses of my eyes grow dim
And lo, the serpent of hatred raises its head in my heart, that serpent that I believe was dead.

Later in this poem Senghor says he crushes the serpent of hatred while looking forward to a new kind of civilization in which all races and cultures will join on a basis of peace, equality and justice. He pleads:

O bless this people that breaks its bonds, O bless this people at bay who face the bulimic pack of bullies and torturers. And with them all the peoples of Europe, all the peoples of Asia, all the peoples of Africa, all the peoples of America who sweat blood and sufferings. And see, in the midst of these millions of waves, the sea-swell of the heads of my people. And grant to their warm hands that they may clasp the earth in a girdle of brotherly hands beneath the Rainbow of Thy Peace.

Historic African figures especially those who resisted the European invasion and were subsequently depicted as outlaws, despots, and/or slave traders in accounts written by colonialists, serve as subjects of poems, novels and dramas by African writers. The story of El Hadj Omar, who fought the invader and "taught Islam from the banks of the Senegal . . . to the banks of the Niger," is related by Ousmane Soce in *Contes et legendes de l'Afrique Noire*. Lat Dior, a Sengelese who continued to resist for twenty years is the hero of Amadou Cisse Dia's drama *Les derniers jours de Lat Dior*. Several novelists and poets write of Chaka, the Zulu warrior and dreaded King owed his military successes to witchcraft, who killed his relatives and even his fiancee in order to advance his own career and increase his own power. In a dramatic poem entitled "Chaka" and dedicated to the Bantu Martyrs of South Africa, Leopold Sedar Senghor gives a different portrait of the hero and explains his actions. To steel himself against the cruel trials to which the Bantu would be subjected by the "Pink Ears", he felt obliged to stifle all emotional and family ties:

> I saw in a dream all the lands to the far corners of the horizon set under the ruler, the set-square, the compass
> Forests mowed down, hills leveled, valleys and rivers in chains.
> I saw the lands to the four corners of the horizon under the grid traced by the twofold iron ways
> I saw the people of the South like an anthill of silence
> At their work. Work is holy, but work is no longer gesture
> Drum and voice no longer make rhythm for the gestures of the seasons. Peoples of the South, in the shipyards, the ports and the mines and the mills
> And at evening segregated in the kraals of misery.
> And the peoples heap up mountains of black gold and red gold and die of hunger.
> I saw one morning, coming out of the mist of the dawn, a forest of wooly heads
> Arms drooping, bellies hollow, immense eyes, and lips calling to an impossible god.
> Could I stay deaf to such suffering, such contempt?

Then when he is accused of intense hatred, Chaka continues:

> It is not hate to love one's people.
> I say there is no peace under arms, no peace under oppression
> No brotherhood without equality. I wanted all men to be brothers.
> I did not hate the Pink Ears. We welcomed them as messengers of the gods, with pleasant words and delicious drinks.
> They wanted merchandise. We gave them: ivory, honey, rainbow pelts.
> Spices and gold, precious stones, parrots and monkeys.
> Shall I speak of their rusty presents, their tawdry beads?
> Yes, in coming to know their buns, I became a mind, suffering became my lot, suffering of the breast and of the spirit.

Probably one of the most bitter denunciations of the effects of colonialism is made by David Diop quoted above. In tones reminiscent of a young Langston Hughes, one of his early poems described "the time of maryrdom":

> The white man killed my father
> My father was proud
> The white man raped my mother
> My mother was beautiful
> The white man beat my brother under the highway sun
> My brother was strong
> The white man turned toward me
> His hands red with black blood
> And in the voice of a Master:
> "Hey Boy! bring me a whiskey, a napkin, and some water!"

In the first five lines of his poem "The Vultures," he says:
> In those days
> When civilization kicked us in the face
> When holy water slapped our cringing brows
>   The vultures built in the shadow of their talons
> The bloodstained monument of tutelage.

This view of the evil, murderous results of European civilization on the lives of Africans finds added expression in the early poems of writers from South Africa. The first Africans who were lured or forced into the mines of South Africa are said to have experienced a special horror going beyond fear of physical destruction. Benedict W. Vilakazi, who was linguist on the staff at Witwatersrand University in Johannesburg, says in "In the mines":

> Thunder away, machines of the mines
> Thunder away from dawn till sunset,
> I will get up soon: do not pester me,
> Thunder away machines. Heed not
> The groans of the black labourers
> Writhing with pains of their bodily wounds
> The air close and suffocating
> With dirt and sweat of their bodies
> As they drain their hips till nothing is left.

* * *

> Those black rock-rabbits without tails
> You caught and stowed away in holes
> To own and milk as yielding cows
>
> Their lungs go rusty and rusty
> and they cough and they lie down and they die
> But you irons, you never cough. I note and wonder why.

POLITICS OF AFRICAN LITERATURE

After referring to the black laborers who are literally imprisoned in the mines as "black field-mice with minds all wrapped," he goes beyond this pathos to strike a note of revolt:

"Wait just a while, for feeble as I seem,
From these same little arms one day
there flew some fierce, long-bladed spears
Which I hurled till the sun was darkened . . .
I was robbed
But still I go on dreaming, son of Iron,
Dreaming that the land of my fathers' fathers
Comes back to the hands of the homeless Blacks!

A different tone is expressed by S. E. Drune Mqhayi, another poet, novelist, essayist and journalist in the early part of the present century. In a poem commemorating the visit to South Africa of the Prince of Wales in 1925 he achieves striking irony using the style of the traditional praise-poem. In "Greeting the British Prince," he says in part:

Ah Britain! Great Britain!
Great Britain of the endless sunshine!
She has conquered the oceans and laid them low;
She has drained the little rivers and lapped them dry,
She has swept the little nations and wiped them away;
And now she is making for the open skies.
She sent us the preacher, she sent us the bottle,
She sent us the Bible and barrels of brandy,
She sent us the breechloader, she sent us cannon.
O Roaring Britain! What must we embrace?
You sent us the truth, denied us the truth;
You sent us the life, deprived us the live;
You sent us the light, we sit in the dark.
Shivering, benighted, in the bright noonday sun.

One of the concomitant results of colonization was the introduction of Christianity to Africa. Hardly one African in ten would fail to affirm the benefits brought to his section of the continent by the missionaries, chief among these would be schools and the idea of the value of education. In general, however, they consider the missionary an ally of the colonialist and they attack his hypocrisy, his segregated church and his sweeping condemnation of African values, which he fails to understand, and the severity of his preachments. Many obviously accepted the new religion for various reasons.

For example in Ferdinand Oyono's novel *Une Vie de Boy* translated as *Houseboy*, the priest believes that it was the Holy Spirit which led to him the little African who became his "boy". Yet Toundi, the "boy", knew differently. He confesses his motive for joining the new religion saying, "I just wanted to get close to the white man with hair like the beard on a maize cob who dressed in woman's clothes and gave little black boys sugar lumps." Toundi's comments on the success of the priest's work continue:

"I was in a gang of heathen boys who followed the missionary about as he went from hut to hut trying to make converts to the new religion. He knew a few words of Ndjem but his pronunciation was so bad that the way he said them, they all had obscene meaning. This amused everybody and his success was assured." The seating arrangement in the Church followed the usual pattern. The best section nearest the altar was cordoned off for the whites. Seated in cane armchairs covered with velvet cushions, they were able to follow the mass comfortably. Men and women sat together shoulder to shoulder. The nave of the church was completely reserved for Africans. "They sit on tree trunks instead of benches and these are arranged in two rows. The faithful are supervised by catechists ready to pounce at the least sign of inattention. These servants to God march up and down the central aisle that divides the men from the women, carrying sticks." The African men and women are taught to deliberately turn their backs when they stand to be sure they don't look at one another. The Catechists watch for the flicker of an eyelid and the guilty are reprimanded and punished.

In *Le Pauvre Christ de Bomba* by Mongo Beti, the priest discovering that the villagers are dancing on the first Friday of the month which is a holy day, wants to punish the whole village. One of the non-Christians tells the priest that he is not a Christian and never shall be. He asks, however, if the priest's reaction was just for blacks or if he would have reacted the same way, breaking musical instruments and condemning the practices of the people if this had been a group of white dancers instead of black. He finally tells the priest that he wishes Jesus Christ himself would come to talk with them as he believes Christ would be more reasonable and tolerant and would give them freedom to dance. The priest is a white man and is incapable of understanding the importance of the dance of the African.

"Prayer and Penitence of a Young Christian" by a young Congolese poet portrays the mocking attitude of many young Africans towards Christianity:

Lord, why have you made this morning so gray, so sad?
Is it because I sinned last night?
Are you that angry Lord?
Even the proud rooster hasn't crowed this morning.
Even the little sparrows haven't crowed this morning.
Even the little sparrows haven't left their nests under the roofs.
Lord, Lord, I've sinned, I confess,
But it's not entirely my fault.
When I looked into her eyes, O Lord,
Those eyes could have made me do anything —
They could have made me eat on Good Friday,
They could have made me disrespect the Holy Father, the Pope.
Lord, Lord, I've sinned, I confess.
I confess, I found her long black, hair more beautiful
    than that of the Virgin Mary.
Oh Lord, I'm ashamed of myself.
Give me the punishment for a sinner,
Have no pity of me.
I recognize my irreparable, my unpardonable, my mortal sin
But Lord, take pity on my uncle
Who needs a good harvest of palm wine for his daughter's dowry.
Take pity on Mama who needs a good harvest of corn and millet.
Lord, I recognize my irreparable, my unpardonable, my mortal sin
But they haven't done any wrong, Lord.
Give them back that bright sun, the joy of their life
Give them back the blue sky that makes them vibrate with love
And give Mama that sunshine that she wants so badly for her
    millet, but
As for me — don't let me live
For I cut Catechism class last Sunday.

Onologeum Lamba, a poet from Mali, notes how easily Africans are accused of the most inhuman crimes by Westerners who do not know them. In his poem, "When Black Teeth Speak", he says:

Folks call me a cannibal
But you know how folks talk
People see my red gums
But does anybody have white gums?
Long live tomatoes!

People say that fewer tourists are coming nowadays
But you know we aren't Americans
And all our folks are broke
People think it's my fault they're afraid
But look! — My teeth are white not red
I haven't eaten anybody

Folks are mean and say I eat cooked tourists
Or perhaps toasted tourists
Cooked or toasted? I asked.
They became silent and looked uneasy
Long live tomatoes!

Everyone knows that an agricultural country goes in for agriculture
Long live vegetables
And everyone contends that vegetables don't keep the farmer alive
And that I'm too husky for a vegetarian
Down with my teeth!

Suddenly people surrounded me and tied me up
And threw me to the ground at the feet of Justice.
Are you a cannibal or not? . . . Answer.
You think you're clever and act proud.
You'll see . . . We'll fix your business!
Do you have any last words?
I yelled . . . "Vivent les tomates"!

People are mean and women are curious, you know
And there was one in the group of the curious
Who cried . . . "Open up his stomach
I'm sure my father's still in there."
And they grabbed the Gillette blade and patiently
Kriss, Krass, Flok. They opened my stomach.
A tomato patch was growing there
Irrigated by streams of palm wine.
Vivent les tomatoes"!

Similar examples of the African writers' satirical treatment of his experiences and of how others characterize him are numerous in the literature. They are simply literary expressions of his desire for independence and equality. To justify this right to equality and independence the African novelist has used a variety of tactics; he has written objectively, subjectively, bitterly, ironically, sympathetically, in protest or defense. He has written autobiographical novels like Camara Laye's *The African Child,* or *Down Second Avenue,* the work of Ezekiel Mphalele, a South African exile. He has written tales of the bush, stories of the miners in Johannesburg or railway strikes in Senegal, tales of the teeming urban centers such as Cyprian Ekwensi's *People of the City* or Chinua Achebe's *No Longer at Ease,* and he has written historical tales and legends about the Old African empires of Ghana, Mali and Songhai. He has written stories of the transplanted African, political novels such as Conton's *The African* or Achebe's *A Man of the People.* He has written of the tragedy of the breaking down of tribal traditions and the weakening of the moral values of the old system in Achebe's excellently written *Things Fall Apart*. And this multiple approach has made his work more readable, has carried his message to different kinds of readers all over the world and has emphasized the human quality of his people. We see the African as he suffers under colonialism, as he fails and succeeds in meeting the many problems independence has brought. We see him at work, at play or at school. We follow the African from birth to burial, stopping en route to learn about his traditions: about age groups and riots and totems and bride price and courtship and marriage, listening to their venerable elders regret the traditions of the past and to the young men debate the problems of the day.

Chinua Achebe, the leading novelist in present day Nigeria, tells about an Osu, a person dedicated to a god, a thing set apart, taboo forever and his children after him. He could neither marry nor be married by the free-born. Camara Laye's father in the *African Child* learns the future from a little black snake and in his latest novel the snake is still there—the same little black snake. His mother, too, had unusual powers that would seem strange; indeed impossible to us.

Along with the magic there is Negritude, consciously or unconsciously, which Leopold Senghor, the chief theoretician of the movement defines as: "The sum total of the black man's cultural values." Reduced to its lowest common denominator as far as the literature of the black man is concerned, it is rhythm, it is defense of those values honored by African tradition and it is humor. In its eyes blackness is no longer a symbol of shame and degredation.

Among the French speaking writers particularly, there are numerous examples of the young student in Paris suffering from a feeling of alienation from his native culture. Being absorbed in French culture, but not entirely accepted as an organic part of French society, the young African feels that he has come to a dead end and longs for the warmth and security of his native environment. He begins to stress his "Africanness," his Negritude and to seek in his past those elements which distinguish him from the Eureopean.

African poetry presents all the familiar themes of Negritude; the pervasive presence of the dead and their guiding influence upon the living; the devastation of ancient Africa and its culture by white Europe; the harsh rigidity of the modern west and its desperate need for the complementing qualities of Africa; the warm triumphant beauty of the African woman.

Any number of poets treat this last theme. In opposition to

Western values and ideals, they pay tribute to the girls and women of their continent. They praise the beauty and grace and commend the stamina and fortitude of women who have long played important roles in their cultures. Martial Sinda of the former French Congo in "Pour une jeune Congolaise" laments that the girls in Paris are too cold, too white and entirely lacking in charm and grace. He declares to his young Congolese girl the beauty he sees when he looks at her:

> Your love warm and sweet as honey
> The black tenderness of your appetizing face.
> Your glance so gay, so quick, gentle, languid, and kind
> Your well shaped breasts
> Your harmonious lips
> Your smooth and glossy skin
> O black woman, how truly beautiful you are in your native dress!

David Diop says in his poem "A une danseuse noire":

> Negro girl, my warm clamor of Africa
> My land of mystery and my fruit of reason
> You are dance by the simple joy of your smile
> By the offerings of your breasts and your secret powers
> You are dance by the golden legends of nuptial nights.

Among the finest of all verse praising the black woman is Leopold Senghor's "Femme Noire", the first, second, and last stanzas of which follow:

> Nude woman, black woman
> Clad in your color which is life
> In your shape which is beauty!
> I have grown big in your shade, and the sweetness of your hands has blinded me.
> Here in the heart of summer and at mid-day
> I find the promised land
> And your beauty strikes me to the heart
> As lightning strikes the eagle.
>
> Naked woman, unknown woman
> Ripe fruit with firm flesh, dark ecstacies of black wine.
> Mouth which makes my mouth lyric
> Savannas of wide horizons, plains trembling under the warm touch of the East winds,
> Carved tom tom, sounding under the conquerors' fingers
> Your grave deep voice is the spiritual song of the Beloved.
> Naked woman, black woman
> Your passing beauty I make eternal
> Before it is turned to ashes by jealous Fate to nourish the roots of life.

Color prejudice and discrimination are as much a part of the African's experience as that of the black man in any other part of the world. The writer's reaction to this phenomenon is largely determined by geography and by the colonial policy that his country has known. David Diop reflects deep mental anguish when he experiences a scornful attitude, as expressed in "Un Blanc m'a dit":

> You are only a Negro
> A Negro
> A dirty Negro
> Your heart is a sponge which drinks —
> Which drinks deliriously the poison of Vice
> And your color imprisons your blood
> Eternally in slavery.

A less vehement but an equally effective expression reflects the experience of Dennis Brutus who was born in Southern Rhodesia and spent much of his life in South Africa until exiled. His recounting of persecution and injustice in South Africa is significant. In "Poem" he says:

> Somehow we survive
>   and tenderness, frustrated, does not wither.
>
> Investigating searchlights rake
>   our naked unprotected contours;
> Over our heads the monolithic decalogue
>   of fascist prohibition glowers
>   and teeters for a catastrophic fall;
>   boots club the peeling door.
> But somehow we survive
>   severance, deprivation, loss.
> Patrols uncoil along the asphalt dark
>   hissing their menace to our lives.
>
> Most cruel, all our land is scarred with terror,
>   rendered inlovely and unlovable;
>   sundered are we and all our passionate surrender
>   but somehow tenderness survives!

How moving is his "Night Song City":

> Sleep well, my love, sleep well;
>   the harbour lights glaze over the restless docks,
>   police cars cockroach through the tunnel streets;
>
>   from the shanties creaking iron sheets
>   violence like a bug-infested rag is tossed
>   and fear is imminent as sound in the wind-swung bell;

>   the long day's anger pants from a sand and rocks;
>   but for this breathing night at least,
>   my land, my love, sleep well.
>
> The sounds begin again;
>   the siren in the night
>   the thunder at the door
>   the shriek of nerves in pain
>
> Then the keening crescendo
>   of faces split by pain
>   the wordless, endless wait
>   only the unfree know.
>
> Importunate as rain
>   the wraiths exhale their woe
>   over the sirens, knuckles, boots;
>   my sounds begin again.

Wole Soyinka, one of the leading dramatists and poets of Nigeria, portrays still another attitude when confronted with racial discrimination. In "The Telephone Conversation" he recounts an event which frequently occurs when an African seeks lodging in England:

> The price seemed reasonable, location
> Indifferent. The landlady swore she lived
> Off premises. Nothing remained
> But self-confession. "Madam" I warned
> 'I have a wasted journey — I am African.'
> Silence. Silenced transmission of
> Pressurized good-breeding. Voice, when it came,
> Lipstick coated, long gold-rolled
> Cigarette-holder pipped. Caught I was foully.
> 'How DARK? — I had not misheard — 'Are
> YOU LIGHT?
> Or VERY DARK?' Buton B. Button
>   A Stench
> Of rancid breath of publichide — and speak.
> Red booth. Red pillar-box. Red double tiered
> Omnibus squelching tar. It was real! Shamed
> by ill-mannered silence, surrender
> Pushed dumbfoundment to beg simplification
> considerate she was, varying the emphasis —
> 'ARE YOU DARK? OR VERY LIGHT?'
> Revelation came.
> 'You mean — like plain or milk chocolate?'
> Her assent was clinical, crushing in its light
> Impersonality. Rapidly, wave-length adjusted,

I chose! 'West African, sepia' and as afterthought,
'Down in my passport.' Silence for spectroscopic
Flight of fancy, till truthfulness changed her accent
Hard on the mouth piece. 'What's that?' conceding
'I don't know what that is! 'Like brunette'
'That's Dark, Isn't It?' 'Not altogether.'
Facially, I am brunette, but Madam, you should see
The rest of me. Palm of my hand, soles of my feet
Are a peroxide blonde. Friction, caused —
Foolishly, Madam — by sitting down, has turned
My bottom raven black — One moment, Madam! '— sensing
Her receiver rearing on the thunderclap
About my ears — 'Madam,' I pleaded, 'Wouldn't you rather
See for yourself?'

One last complaint of the African concerns the confrontation of his traditions with Western ideals. This is very serious as it attacks his very identity. Roland Dempster, one of Liberia's poets, objects to the attempts of Westerners to remake the African in the Western image.

I am not you.
But you will not give me a chance
If I were you —
But you will not let me be me.
You meddle, interfere in my affairs
But you know I'm not you
As if they were yours and you were me.
You're unfair, unwise to think I can
Be you, talk, act and think like you.
God made you — you
For God's sake let me be me.

Mr. Dempster calls the poem "African's Plea" and what he pleads for is spelled out in greater detail by other African authors, for example, by Wole Soyinska, Nigeria's most popular playwright who had three plays produced with much success in New York some years ago. In the play *The Lion and the Jewel* the author, ridiculing his compatriots who imitate Western ways, has one of his characters, a school teacher say to a beautiful girl, whom he loves but has failed to impress:

It's never any use.
Bush-girl you are, bush-girl you'll always be;
Uncivilized and primitive — bush-girl!
I kissed you as all educated men—
And Christians — kiss their wives.
It is the way of civilized romance.

The young lady, unmoved by the "civilized" western ways of the young teacher, mocks him, saying that he is only trying to avoid paying the lawful bride-price for her. Later he promises her:

> Within a year or two, this town will see a transformation.
> Bride-price will be a thing forgotten
> And wives shall take their place by men.

He continues to dream of the future when "progress" will have introduced modern Western ways:

> A motor road will pass this spot and bring the city ways to us.
> The ruler shall ride cars, not horses
> Or a bicycle at least.
> We'll print newspapers everyday with pictures of seductive girls.
> The world will judge our progress by the girls who win beauty contests.
> Where is our school of Ballroom dancing?
> We must be modern with the rest of the world
> Or live forgotten by the world.
> We must reject the palm wine habit
> And take to tea, with milk and sugar.

A poet from Mali, Ouologuem Yambo presents a wife scolding her husband who has been brain-washed by the West. In "A Mon Mari" the man has been so steeped in French culture that his wife no longer recognizes him as the man she married. First, he changes his name; he used to be Bimbirokak, he loved his wife; they enjoyed eating their native food together; they were very happy. But now he has become Victor-Emile-Louis-Henri-Joseph; he has stopped eating African food and wearing African clothing. At the end of the poem the wife complains: "Formerly, I was underdeveloped; but thanks to you, I have become undernourished."

Many writers have attacked the French colonial policy of banning the speaking of local African languages in the schools. This practice sometimes led to amusing results as in an incident related by a Cameroonian novelist concerning the celebration of the French Independence Day, July 14. In the presence of their parents and the French officials the pupils sang "La Marseillaise" and the parents were proud and convinced that their children were singing in French while the French were equally certain that the children were singing in the African language. The author assures his readers that it was neither French no African.

> Flight of fancy, till truthfulness changed her scent
> Hard on the mouthpiece. 'What's that?' conceding
> 'I don't know what that is'! 'Like brunette'.

'That's Dark, Isn't It?' 'Not altogether.
Facially, I am brunette, but Madam, you should see
The rest of me. Palm of my hand, soles of my feet
Are a peroxide blonde. Friction, caused —
Foolishly Madam — by sitting down, has turned
My bottom raven black — one moment Madam'! — sensing
Her receiver rearing on the thunderclap
About my ears — 'Madam,' I pleaded, 'wouldn't you rather
See for yourself?'

This is an excellent example of biting humor handled lightly and artistically.

It would be unfair and unjust on my part to terminate this essay leaving the impression that all African literature has a social mission or that the writers are so preoccupied with their problems that they cannot produce reflective or meditative literature with no other purpose than to create art. To dispel such a thought one has only to read "Homecoming" by Lenria Peters of Gambia, "Requiem" by Soyinka, "For Granny", "Night Rain", or "Ibadan" by John Pepper Clark to mention only a few examples.

How do we see the African through his writings? How does he see himself? How does he think others see him? If we take the various views drawn from his literary works he is a complex person with as many facets to his character and mind as any other complex human. In his "Prayer to Masks" Leopold Senghor paints one portrait of this being:

Now while the Africa of despotism is dying — it is the agony of
    a pitiable princess
Just like Europe to whom she is connected through the navel,
Now turn your immobile eyes towards your children who have
    been called
And who sacrifice their lives like the poor man his last garment
So that hereafter we may cry 'here' at the rebirth of the world
    being the heaven that the white flour needs.
For who else would teach rhythm to the world that has died of
    machines and cannons?
For who else should ejaculate the cry of joy, that arouses the
    dead and the wise in a new dawn?
Say, who else could return the memory of life to men with a torn
    hope?
They call us cotton heads, and coffee men, and oily men,
They call us men of death!
But, we are the men of the dance whose feet only gain power
    when they beat the hard soil.

This is one side of the African as seen by one of the Continent's best-known poets. There are many views and opinions expressed in this rapidly growing body of interesting and worthwhile literature which reflects the soul and human condition of a people. Hundreds of other examples could be given of what the African is as portrayed by his writers. But why not accept the advice of Soyinka in the "Telephone Conversation" and judge for yourself!

PASSION AND POETRY
IN THE WORKS OF DENNIS BRUTUS
by
Pol Ndu

The word passion immediately calls to mind tremendous suffering. Such a high degree of suffering could be occasioned by severe loss, by great mental or physical pain, or an alienating spiritual upheaval. If the high degree of suffering sustains over an extended length of time, a disintegration of the suffering body may precede a chastisement of the enduring spirit. That was the case in Christ's passion. We are told that when His chastised spirit left His body, that is, when His flesh disintegrated, darkness came over the earth, graves opened and ghostly noises filled the air. Three days later, He reappeared, complete and superhuman.

But passion could equally connote emotion: the surging out of sentiment towards an appreciable circumstance, an object or an idea. When Wordsworth gasped "To The Cuckoo"

   O blithe newcomer! I have heard,
     I hear thee and rejoice,
   O Cuckoo! shall I call thee bird,
     Or but a wandering voice?

his passion was suddenly flushed towards the familiar music of the bird which kept floating back to him over several years. And that reminiscence brought him joy.

Passion of sorrow as in Christ's and passion of joy as in Wordsworth's are necessary ingredients for great poetry. When these passions are effectively and adequately experienced, the result is either a destruction of the tortured personality and the emergence of a chastised thing, fierce but delicious or the emergence of this fierce thing in the form of some immortal accomplishment. Sylvia Plath was tortured by the loss of her father, by the instability of her married life, by the brutality of an insensitive mankind. By the age of 25, she was 'like a woman on fire', producing two, three, six complete poems night after night. Her fire was black and its name was hatred. Her works were hard and small like missiles, and they were flung with flat force

> Now I break up in pieces that fly
>   about like clubs.
> A wind of such violence
> Will tolerate no bystandings: I must shriek.

But beneath the hatred she fanned fear:

> I am terrified by this dark thing
> that sleeps in me;
> All day I feel its soft, feathery turnings,
>   its malignity . . .
> What is this, this face
> So murderous in its strangle of branches?

And beneath the fear, she found a sinister love of death. She longed to feel

> the knife not carve, but enter
> Pure and clean as the cry of a baby,
> And the Universe slide from my side

Finally Sylvia executed what a critic had called her "Last unwritten poem" — suicide; capping it with a clouting couplet:

> The blood jet is poetry
> There is no stopping it.[1]

I have taken time to quote Sylvia's case because it has some bearing with my idea of passion and poetry. Sylvia Plath is dead, having undergone the excruciating physical and mental torture. But she lives in *The Colossus, Ariel,* "Daddy," "Lady Lazarus" and *The Bell Jar.* Her bibliography is modest, but the quality is superb. In the poems leading to her subsequent suicide, she had succeeded in crystalising in concrete terms all her fury, hatred and love.

This success results from an uninhibited resignation to the forces of torture with a love that though macabre, is deeply genuine.

Dennis Brutus sows the needs of great poetry when he discusses themes of special intimacy to himself. Such themes could have arisen from some loss, some desire, some feeling or even the pain of the confrontation of the abominable regime. But in each case, the poet does not generalize or pose as the mouthpiece of a doomed race. He speaks from the labyrinths of his fear, his anger, the wells of his thirst. This is only when the two strands of passion are consumated in him and he knows that if oppression takes

> Out the poetry and fire
> or watch it ember out of sight
> sanity reassembles its ash
> the moon relinquishes the night.
> But here and here remain the scalds
> a sudden turn or breath may ache,
> and I walk on cindered pasts
> for thought or hope (what else?) can break.[2]

The revulsion and terror of the poet as "police cars cockroach through the tunnel streets;

> from shanties creaking iron-sheets
> violence like a bug-infested rag is tossed
> and fear is immanent as sound in the windswung bell

is self expletive. Or when

> The sounds begin again;
> the siren in the night
> the thunder at the door
> the shriek of nerves in pain.
>
> Then the keening crescendo
> of faces split by pain
> the wordless; endless wail
> only the unfree know.
>
> ———
>
> my sounds begin again
> (Sirens Boots Knucles)

one does not need to be told that a great mind is facing a great upheaval. The words are familiar enough, but they are so selected and worked to a decrescendo that when 'his' sounds begin again the reader has tasted the bitter dregs of the poet's ordeal, but with a fresh determination. Each dominant word is loaded with poetic responsibility and meaning and a great intensity is achieved. This is of course because as I have said, the poet is writing from instances of direct personal import. He does not write to postulate some moral, philosophical, political theory or slogan. He is merely expressing his terror in the language of poetry.

> These are not images to cheer you
> — except that you may see in these small acts
> some evidence of my thought and caring:
> but still I do not fear their power to wound

> knowing your grief, your loss and anxious care,
> rather I send you bits to fill
> the mosaic of your calm and patient knowledge
> — picking jagged bits embedded in my mind —
> partly to wrench some ease for my own mind.
> And partly that some world some time may know
> (Letters to Martha: Postscripts 1)[3]

It is interesting to note that Brutus does pick jagged bits embedded in his mind "partly" to "wrench some ease" for his mind. I would substitute principally for "partly". But whichever way, the ease of mind is only wrenched when pains and passions are manfully indulged. In this indulgence, the poet should face up his punishment with a relish that must necessarily astound the uninitiated.

> More terrible than any beast
> that can be tamed or bribed
> the iron monster of the world
> ingests me in its grinding maw:
>
> agile as ballet-dancer
> fragile as butterfly
> I egg-dance with numble wariness
> —stave off my fated splintering.
> (Sirens Boots Knucles)

Man's life is brittle as the butterfly's, fragile as an egg and in the jaws of the grinding "iron monster" the poet realises that his destruction is gradual but systematic. It is pathetic and frightening. He must do something. But

> Time — ordinary time —
> exerts its own insistent
> unobstrusive discipline.

The beauty of these lines will certainly be watered down by any attempts at explication. Time is certainly "ordinary" but only to the free. To the unfree, every minute seems an eternity, an eternity of waiting, longing and pining.

In these very personal poems, Dennis Brutus leads every reader deep down into the turbulence of his imagination. The reader becomes both spectator and participant in the tragic drama taking place there. The passion of sorrow for being considered sub-human in a basically human world, and the passion of pleasure for sustaining life through the vicissitudes of the deadly hostilities are merged and fine poetry is the synthetic result. But as soon as the poet takes the propagandist rostrum, poetry flies and what follows might be moving but never profound. In "Mirror Sermon I",

> Our images cavort
> in silent dissonance
> Or graceless dance
> slow sarabands of passionless lasciviousness
> and lace through a cacophonous gavotte.
>   Marionettes
> devoid of graceful antecedents
> we pirouette
> in senseless choreography ...
>   (Sirens Boots Knucles)

obsolete and almost out of the way 'ballet-dance' terms are incongruously strung together to lament the helplessness of the South African "marionettes". 'Cavort', 'sarabands', 'cacaphonous gavotte', 'pirouette', 'choreography' make indeed a

> cold reflection
> of our interlocking nudity

which seems to moralise

> ascetically
> on sensual intellection
> or morality

and one begins to wonder whether the guilt of the "cold reflection" in "sensual intellection" and "sensual morality" is the poet's or still that of his white oppressors.

When the passions are not completely experienced in a poet, his poetry is jagged often sentimental and intruding. That unusual fuse which breaks a poem into the highest orbits of the imagination and the deepest layers of feeling is absent. In the several works of Dennis Brutus, these passions have not been fully reconciled. His lot is quite a pitiable and pitful one. Hunted from pillar to post by an abominable regime, thrown into jail as often as he is caught, banned from the exercise of the simplest and most elementary rights of man — to talk and to write — separated for a time from a cherished family, he is still something of a dilettante. His bitterness remains mostly unresolved. He argues in "Their Behavior." (Letters to Martha, p. 28)

> Their guilt
>   is not so very different from ours
>   — who has not joyed in the arbitrary exercise of power
>   or grasped for himself what might have been another's
>   and who has not used superior force in the moment
>   when he could
>   (and who of us has not been tempted to these things?) —

Brutus here attempts to be profound but his argument does not quite click. It sounds like an inconclusive yardstick of anti-Marxist: Apartheid could be tolerated because, given the same circumstances as the whites, the blacks would practise apartheid. This is as untrue as it is begging the question. And because of the posturing, Brutus only succeeds in making plain unpoetic statements. He apparently wants to fight. But his fight must not be bitter. It is not a fight of life and death — for him. It is the mercenary soldier's fight: gradual, curious but most cautious.

It is not the same with Mphahlele who asks 'You want to know?' in Death.[4]

>My mother died at 45
>at 42 my brother followed.
>You want to know?
>She cleaned the houses of the white folk
>and washed their bodily dirt
>out of the baths.
>. . . . .
>My grandma left at 80
>she also washed her years away
>and saw them flow
>into the drain
>with the white man's scum.
>Many more from our tree have fallen —
>known and unknown.
>. . . . . *and that white colossus*
>he was butchered by a man
>they say is mad
>. . . . .
>a tyrant dead is not enough!
>Vengeance is mine and yours and his,
>says the testament of man
>nailed to the boulder of pain
>*and they say the butcher's mad*
>*who sank the knife into the tyrants neck*
>*while the honourable men*
>*who rode his taks of fire*
>*looked on.*

The irony is clear. But it bites terribly deep. The poor butcher who eliminates a colossal tyrant is branded mad while the tyrants' ministers of death are 'honourable'. In any case, they are indeed 'honourable' since their honour and office would not combat or comprehend this new madness. The butcher is mad, and as armed guards looked on, dazed and full of 'honour', he walked up the aisle and mowed down the colossus of a tyrant from his height of power. Only after the deed were the guards awakened and

> to kill a bug
> they set a house on fire
> to kill a fire
> they flood a country
> to save a country
> drench the land in blood
> to peg the frontiers of their colour madness

But these same people do not live above the mess of their bloody involvement. They do not exist outside the frontiers of their flooded country. And immediately one feels that these giants pursuing a chicken are bound to fall, and their fall bound to be a tragic fall into an inferno of a raging bloody country.

> .... *and we laughed and danced*
> *when news came of the death of that colossus*
> *— the death of a beast of prey.*

This is a different brand of protest. It is not protest harping sensitively on the very fine sophistics of modern man. Nor is it protest rejecting the rewarding attributes of refinement. But protest asserting the inescapable certainty of regard: whether of good with good or of evil with evil.

> You want to know?
> because I nourish
> a deadly life within
> my madness shall have blood.

At last, the butcher's madness has become the poet's madness which of course will have blood because in his Karmic logic of reward, blood will have blood. Much as Brutus' anti-Marxist theory of universal bent to greed might sound intellectual, the practical realities of the South African situation needs a realistic and grim facing up, a combat. The anti-apartheid fighter could lose the battle in the short run, even lose his life, but at the moment of death, he should realize a special expiation and satisfaction, a traumatic canonization. It is this final leap into sainthood which Brutus severally refuses or fears

> After the sentence
> mingled feelings:
> sick relief,
> . . . . .
> vague heroism
> mixed with self-pity
> and tempered by the knowledge of those

>   who endure much more
>   and endure . . . .
>   (Letters to Martha I)

This unsuccessful counterposing of the commonplace "mixed feelings" and "vague heroism" is unfortunate. It is not the feeling of Mphahlele's madman. Even Brutus himself knows this, for he names the impure item in his experience as 'self pity'. This impure "self pity" blunts the edge of his language and emasculates his poetry. He is cowed down by an "awareness of the proximity of death", and having handed in "nails and screws and other sizable bits of metals" he falls to his knees in the "childhood habit of nightly prayers" perhaps remembering the great Christian precept of "Blessed are the meek .. ." Even when this meek child cries for vengeance, it is the cry of a toothless cur, there is no sharpness, there is no weapon; the cry is within him and muffled there.

>   . . . . .
>   . . . . .
>   but our concern
>   is how they hasten or delay
>   a special freedom —
>   that of those the prisons hold
>   and who depend on change
>   to give them liberty
>
>   And so one comes to a callousness,
>   a savage ruthlessness —
>   voices shouting in the heart
>   "Destroy! Destroy!
>   "Let them die in thousands!"
>   really it is impatience
>   (Letters to Martha II)

But they never die, not even in fives and tens, because the voices shout only "in the heart" and if evil comes upon some men the way others wish it, very few, if any people will be alive the next minute. What 'Change' actually do those in the prisons depend on for liberty? A change of mind of the South African whites? That would be a miracle in the 20th century. A change of government by a revolution or a coup d'etat? The only 'change' that can effectively alter the human tragedy in South Africa is that which gives the 'coloured' man his due place as human. For Brutus, this change will be far in coming,

>   . . . . .

> So one grits to the burden
> and resolves to doggedly endure
> the outrages of prison
>
> (Letters to Martha 13)

realising that

> we were simply prisoners
> of a system we had fought
> and still opposed
> (Letters to Martha 14)

In an article *Protest Against Apartheid* Dennis Brutus himself states that his 'case is not an extreme one' and he catalogues the series of bans and restrictions that had been placed on him. "In fact, my Banning Order (which has Mr. Voster's autograph!) specifically forbids me to compose slogans so that, in fact, even a string of words could have been illegal". I wonder whose 'case' could be more extreme! Then he continues "I think one may say in all seriousness that to write at all once you are banned from writing — and it doesn't matter whether you write badly — constitutes a form of protest against apartheid in South Africa."[5] This is true. But it is not all the truth. It matters very much how well you write, and how much you protest because the power of the written word is onerous and immense. And if the devil can cite the scriptures to support devilry, it is the ambiguous and equivocal sections that he could cite. Thus Brutus decided to start his classification of protesters with "Alan Paton who represents one extreme of protest literature in South Africa, and then work slowly over to some one like Alex la Guma who represents the other extreme. In between, you will find today people like Nadine Gordimer, and in terms of drama, Athol Fugard."[6] Brutus condemns Paton as a white sympathizer and Nadine Gordimer as an insensitive, cold machine, without "warmth and feeling." But Athol Fugard's *The Blood Knot* he says "cleverly approached it [apartheid] from both angles — it is both conflict and unity — for the white and the black are, as often they are in South Africa, blood brothers. One has turned out to be black, and the other one has turned out to be white."[7] This is the pampered philosophy of the weaker man's live and let live. For the South African tragedy does not deserve so much understanding. If the white and the black in South Africa are so much blood brothers, meant to cooperate peacefully perpetually, why do some noble non-whites eventually decide to quit the cherished compromise into exile? Brutus himself for instance.

The salient point is that blood is blood. Pathologists have shown that all blood at best is the same. If therefore at any point or place some people want to show that their 'blood' is more blood than the blood of others, they have to be condemned, in unequivocal terms and when possible, in the language of Mphahlele's madman. The basic plague of the white South African is his feeling that white is the colour of the gods. The normal human being will readily acknowledge the differences between himself and others in terms of intellect, status, education or achievement. But there is no apology for anyone who refuses to accept his intellectual or social equal or even superior on the basis of colour. This is why protest writers in Africa have to be re-classified and delineated into those who regard the South African tragedy as normal and acceptable and those who regard it as abnormal, inimical and unpardonable in society. This is what John Povey partly does in "Profile of an African Artist" where, I think, he also sees Brutus as an artist who considers apartheid evil but pardonable. "Throughout Brutus' poetry" he says "runs an infinite and continuous love for his sad yet beautiful country." In Povey's terms then, Brutus' pathetic love for his country is love to a fault because being human, his love should remain finite even if nostalgic. Infinity should be left to divinity. Povey poses the question "what can the place of innocence and intimacy of human love be here, in a situation that requires a different dedication and loyalty" and answers that "to love a woman seems personal to the point of self-indulgence, an abdication of principle; and yet to Brutus that real tenderness is always urgent."[8] If "that real tenderness" is ever urgent to Brutus and Professor Povey knows that its insistence is an abdication of principle, I also feel that Brutus' indulgence is narcissistic and could have far reaching unwelcome consequences for himself. It is however interesting that Professor Povey regards the rest of Brutus' poetry as contradicting his stated view that

under jackboots our bones and spirits crunch.

It is equally contradictory for Professor Povey to hold that Brutus' optimism is not delusive despite the obvious implication of delusion in his poetry. Such optimism could in fact sustain Brutus' survival, but can never sustain equity or the hope for it in South Africa. Brutus and Company "had fought" the system and probably lost but the 'still' continuous opposition is what I have called the 'mercenary' soldier's battle: gradual, curious but most cautious — because, if Brutus lost his fight, he left no immortal marks whereby any passerby might pause and say "ah! a mortal combat took place here." If the battle was lost, it was lost too early. This probably

PASSION AND POETRY IN DENNIS BRUTUS

means that Brutus has not fully utilized the weapons or the abilities at his disposal. Since he still lives and opportunities still abound, one would expect to see him back in the fray with fresh vigour, greater resolve and very serious weapons.

> Quite early one reaches a stage
> where one resolves to embrace
> the status of prisoner
> with all it entails,
> savouring to the full its bitterness
> and seeking to escape nothing:
>
> . . . . .
> . . . . .
>
> Later one changes
> tries the dodges,
> seeks the easy outs
>
> But the acceptance
> once made
> deep down
> remains.
> (Letters to Martha 16)

The emasculating and pervading influence of self pity still holds down the protagonist. He must break through the shells of the deep-laid 'acceptance' and though refusing "to escape nothing"; refuse also to try the "dodges" and the "easy outs" but decisively "take up arms" against the sea of troubles and quell them by facing them. I do not mean here that Brutus should turn out the proverbial Don Quixote and catch the bull by the horns with bare hands. Instead, he should allow his true nature to take possession of his poetry of the whites' inhumanity to the blacks in South Africa; his nature which feels a sickly revulsion at the "bleak hostility", at the

> Coprophilism, necrophilism; fellatic;
> penis-amputation;
> . . . in this gibbering society . . .
> Suicide, self-damnation . . .
> not to be shaken off.
> (Letters to Marth 5)

Until this true nature takes possession, the passion for sorrow and the passion for joy will not be reconciled in Dennis Brutus' poetry and he shall not have received the bitter baptism of torture which such great poets receive.

In an article "Of Mr. Booker T. Washington and Others" W. E. B. DuBois talks of categories of the critics of Mr. Booker

Washington's approach to the racial impasse in Southern United States. One group, notably of Bowen, Kelley Miller and the Grimkes "acknowledge Mr. Washington's invaluable service in counselling patience and courtesy in (his) demands . . . but they also know and the nation knows, that relentless colour prejudices is more often a cause than a result of the Negro's degradation, they seek the abatement of this relic of barbarism, and not its systematic encouragement and pampering by all agencies of social power from the Associated Press to the Church of Christ . . . they are absolutely certain that the way for a people to gain respect is not by continually belittling and ridiculing themselves, that, on the contrary, Negroes must insist continually, in season and out of season . . . that colour discrimination is barbarism and that black boys need education as well as white boys . . . In failing thus to state plainly and unequivocally the legitimate demands of their people, even at the cost of opposing an honoured leader, the thinking classes of American Negroes would shirk a heavy responsibility."[9] The responsibility of the Negro thinking classes cannot in this circumstance be more onerous than that of South African black or coloured thinkers and writers. The South African black or coloured man who has the opportunity should shriek, even turn militant and use all available machinations to undermine the invidious regime. In a barbarian society, only the laws of the jungle hold.

If *Letters To Martha* is unsuccessful it is because the poet has not fused the reality of his bitter experiences effectively with his poetry. Or, where the poet feels fulfilled, the feeling is insincere. So, he puts down quite often, "phrases and aphorisms" and commonplaces that are quite touching and pitiful but not exquisite.

Great poetry always surfaces from the deepest layers the poets seat of judgement. In this mental arena, the activating agent is absorbed into a mesh of reasonings, and associations are established. The associations utilise metaphors, similes, parables, where effect is sought in the likeness of things; antithesis and contrast, where effect is sought in the unlikeness of things. Such associations are abrupt and rather distinctive. In cases where effect is sought in emphasis, the associations utilise gradation, climax, tone and intensity. This is why Wordsworth's view "that some of the most interesting parts of the best poems will be found to be strictly the language of prose when prose is well written"[10] needs to be restated. It is obvious that an emphasis of structure stronger than that of ordinary expression of words as in poetry necessitates an emphasis stronger than that of the ordinary expression of thought.

> But,
>> Somehow we survive
>> and tenderness frustrated, does not wither.
>> . . . . .
>> . . . . .
>> patrols uncoil along the asphalt dark
>> hissing their menace to our lives,
>
>> most cruel, all our land is scarred with terror;
>> rendered unlovely and unloveable;
>> sundered are we and all our passionate surrender
>
>> but somehow tenderness survives

Paul Theroux in his "Study of Six African Poets" talks of Brutus' great faith in tenderness. "Here is tenderness without rage, but more often it is a mixture of rage and tenderness that prevails in Brutus' poems,"[11] he writes. Though this appraisal is fairly ambivalent one gets the impression from the racy article that Theroux is sympathetic with Brutus' self-pity.

Gerald Moore uses the poem again in "The Claims of the Present" but he explores a different angle from Theroux. He sees the poet's fulfilment as an artist through pain and experience. "Here" he says "the lunge and hiss of tyranny do not shatter the texture of the poem, leaving us again face to face with "the journalistic fact." And poetry interposes itself, not to diminish our pain, but to remind us that even in this extremity man can be something more than an object or a fugitive."[12] Here then we see that Moore is concerned about the 'journalistic fact' which has done harm to much of Brutus' poetry, suffused with self-pity. But in places where Brutus allows passion and poetry to flush each other, we have been left at last with a real hero, an avenged hero, whether his instrument is the tongue or the sword. But it is significant to note that what survives the extremity is always "more than an object or a fugitive." It has to be.

"The diction of poetry could not then be the same with that of prose, . . . and that the great abundance of metaphor or antithesis is displeasing [in prose] because it is not called for by, and interferes with the continuousness of its flow."[13] Poetry therefore which uses little or none of the known poetic devices does not get off the prosaic plane and when prose is loaded with imagery and symbolism as in Carlyle's, it is definitely classed as poetic.

As Hopkins said of Tennyson, Brutus' "gift of utterance is truly golden but go further home and you come to thoughts [and images] commonplace and wanting in nobility, it is genius uninformed by character"[14] because the poet has not resolved his passions well enough to press out from his mills the relevant imagery and symbolism he needs to produce great poetry. In the few places he resolves these passions, Brutus definitely shows great promise.

NOTES

1. See *Time*: The Weekly News Magazine, Vol. 87, No. 23, June 10, 1966, p. 59.
2. *Sirens Boots Knucles* Mbari: Ibadan, 1963.
3. *Letters to Martha and other poems from a South African Prison* Heinemann: London, 1969, p. 20.
4. *Journal of the New African Literature and the Arts,* Stanford, No. 3, Spring 1957, 36-38.
5. Dennis Brutus, "Protest Against Apartheid" in *Protest and Conflict in African Literature,* edd. Cosmo Pieterse and D. Munro, Heinemann: London 1969, pp. 93-100.
6. *Protest and Conflict in African Literature,* p. 95.
7. *Ibid.,* p. 98.
8. John Povey, "Profile of An African Artist," *Journal of the New African Literature and The Arts,* Stanford, No. 3, Spring 1967, pp. 95-100.
9. W. E. B. DuBois, "Of Mr. Booker T. Washington and Others" in *Souls of Black Folk,* Longmans: London 1965, pp. 35-36.
10. Wordsworth, "Preface to the Second Edition of the Lyrical Ballads (1800)," in *Anthology of Romanticism,* 3rd Edition, ed. E. Bernabaum, New York, 1948, p. 300.
11. Paul Theroux 'Study of Six African Poets" in *Introduction to African Literature,* ed. Ulli Beier, Longmans: Nigeria 1964, pp. 110-111.
12. Gerald Moore, *The Chosen Tongue,* Longmans: London, 1969, p. 211.
13. G. M. Hopkins: "Poetic Diction", in *Journals and Papers of G. M. Hopkins,* ed. H. House and G. Storey, Oxford, June 1948, p. 38.
14. W. A. M. Peters, *G. M. Hopkins,* Oxford, June 1948, p. 38.

ACHEBE'S "THINGS FALL APART": AN IGBO NATIONAL EPIC
by
CHARLES E. NNOLIM

If we are still in agreement that the narrative of the epic is a complex synthesis of the cultural, religious, and national experiences of a particular nation or civilization, and that in the national character which emerges from an epic there must be something of estimable fundamental human value behind it all — perhaps heroism, perhaps nobility, perhaps fidelity to a cause worth pursuing, worth struggling for, and worth suffering defeat for — then *Things Fall Apart* could be read as an Igbo Epic, and Okonkwo, the Igbo Epic hero.

It is part of epic irony that out of human limitations, out of human failure, comes confirmation of the fundamental worth of the personality of the nation. In its tragic dimension *Things Fall Apart* seems to be modelled on that celebrated Anglo-Saxon Epic, *Beowulf,* although it at the same time shares certain basic affinities with other classical epics like Homer's the *Odyssey* and Virgil's the *Aeneid.* As in *Beowulf* there lurks in *Things Fall Apart* certain persistent elements in Anglo-Saxon thinking like *Wyrd* (Fate) which destined Okonkwo and the Spirit of Igbo Clanship to die, so that both are *fey,* or fated to die. And as in *Beowulf,* it is with a certain awe, even terror, that one watches the weaving of the complex web of Fate as it unfolds, and one sees with a sense of history the inevitability of destruction and the value of what is lost.

Since the final focus and attention of the epic is on national involvement, the epic hero is bound to be projected as the most vigorous embodiment of the nation's strengths and weaknesses, and through his near-perfect realization of that nation's ideals, his destiny and that of the nation are inextricably interwoven.

Things Fall Apart is a folk epic with that sense of the "tragic-epic" about it which is shared in common with other folk epics. As in other folk epics there is here a nostalgic reflection on the heroic past in which is seen a greatness forever lost to mankind. This is the sense imparted to us as we follow the mind of Okonkwo in the final pages of the book:

> As he lay on his bamboo bed he thought about the treatment he had received in the white man's court, and he swore vengeance. If Umuofia decided on war, all would be well. But if they chose to be cowards he would go out and avenge himself. He thought about wars in the past. The noblest, he thought, was the war against Isike. . . .
>
> "Worthy men are no more," Okonkwo sighed as he remembered those days. "Isike will never forget how we slaughtered them in that war. We killed twelve of their men and they killed only two of ours. Before the end of the fourth market week they were suing for peace. Those were days when men were men."

For full appreciation of Okonkwo as an epic hero, a quick glance at some celebrated heroes of epic literature may prove helpful. The Greek ideal was a man who owed it to himself, his gods and his nation the development of his talents to the highest possible limits. He is individualistic in his pursuit of honor — either in military glory through great feats of valor performed in battle, or in Olympic games where he would win the olive bough not for leading a team to victory but for being the best all-around athlete. Achilles and Odysseus embody these characteristics. The Roman ideal is the Ciceronian concept, fully embodied in Aeneas, of the altruistic hero who puts the good of the state before his own welfare, who is "more ready to endanger his own than the public welfare," and for whom it is not enough to offer his life for his country but also to stake his reputation as well. Beowulf, as the ideal Anglo-Saxon hero, was not only a good swimmer (to go "a-viking" or on piratical excursions was a good Anglo-Saxon "pastime") but under the law of *Wergyld* was also one who successfully avenged wrongs done his kinsman. Mostly all epic heroes are great warriors.

In the light of the foregoing Okonkwo as an epic hero will now be examined. It is now established that in the absence of hereditary kingship, Igbo society was governed by a group of hand-picked self-achievers so that the ideal to which the Igbos tended was the individual whose position in society rests on solid personal achievements. To succeed, or not to succeed; that was the question confronting every Igbo man. For Okonkwo as for many an Igbo man, the fear of failure is a hauntingly tangible thing. Achebe as the speaking omniscient voice has, in many scattered comments laid the background against which Okonkwo struggled — the Igbo values which acted as a touchstone against which success or failure of Igbo manhood was measured. We have such authorial comments as: "Fortunately, among these pepole, a man was judged according to his worth and not according to the worth of his father"; "Age was respected among his people but achievement was revered. As the elders said, if a child washed his hands, he could eat with kings. Okonkwo had clearly washed his hands and so he ate with kings and elders"; "As our people say, a man who pays respect to the great paves the way for his own greatness."

Then Achebe sketches his hero, Okonkwo, as one measuring up to this ideal. He is the embodiment of Igbo tribal aspirations and one whom the Igbo could take up by the hand and lifting it shout in typical Igbo parlance: "There goes Okonkwo, our man. If you see him, you have seen all of us!" Okonkwo was a successful warrior (a trait he undoubtedly shares with Achilles, Odysseus, Aeneas, Beowulf, Kinf Arthur, Charlemagne) and a champion wrestler worthy to be dispatched to Mbaino on a mission of war. Here was a man disadvantaged from birth (his father was a loafer who even made a mess of dying — the achievement-oriented Igbos would not give burial to one lazy enough to allow himself to die of the swelling sickness or kwashiokor which indicates inability to feed oneself) whose fame had "grown like a bushfire in the harmattan"; who "seemed to walk on springs as if he was going to pounce on somebody. And he did pounce on people quite often"; who "in Umuofia's latest war . . . was the first to bring home a human head"; who "was a wealthy farmer and had two barns full of yams, and had just married his third wife"; and whose "life had been ruled by a great passion — to become one of the lords of the clan. That had been his life-spring. And he had all but achieved it."

But then his fears, unfortunately, came to be realized — especially his fear of failure. But the author again spells out what these fears were: "It was the fear of himself, lest he should be found to resemble his father"; his fear that Nwoye would grow up to resemble Unoka, being "possessed by the fear of his father's contemptible life and shameful death"; his fear of displaying any emotion unless it be the emotion of anger, because, "to show affection was a sign of weakness; the one thing worth demonstrating is strength"; the paranoid fear that drove him to cut down Ikemefuna who had called him father because "he was afraid of being thought weak." All these make him the true Igbo national hero, and as was mentioned in the opening paragraphs, it is sometimes out of human limitation, out of human failure that the fundamental worth of the personality of the nation is delineated and defined. There is a piece of Okonkwo in every Igbo man whether he is preparing to take the *Ozo* title or preparing to take his orals for the Ph.D. (the new passport to elitism, the new symbol of achievement). The Igbo in a figurative and literal sense is a wrestler all his life.

One of the evident, though unexplored, affinities which *Things Fall Apart* shares with the classical epic is the geographical distance covered by the epic hero during which he is either on a temporary or permanent exile from his native country. Odysseus was in exile for ten years, Aeneas sojourned to Italy and never returned. Beowulf voyaged to the kingdom of the Danes and later returned to rule Geatland in his turn. Okonkwo was forced into exile in Mbanta for seven years. And it is during the period in exile that the epic hero suffers trials and tribulations (physical or psychological) as he is relentlessly pursued by an offended god or goddess: Odysseus was dogged by Poseidon, Aeneas by Juno, and Okonkwo, I contend, by *Ani*, the Earth goddess.

Okonkwo had offended the Earth-goddess in several ways and as she turns into an avenging goddess, Okonkwo becomes, as the Igbos say it, *"Onye agwu n'eso"* — one whose footsteps are dogged by Agwu, the twin-sister of *Ani*, the Earth-goddess, or rather, her avenging spirit. It is my contention that the misfortunes which befall Okonkwo were not solely unmotivated but were the result of Okonkwo's offenses against the Earth-goddess which became an avenging fury and marked down Okonkwo as *fey* (fated to die). Achebe is too careful an artist not to provide motivations for what happened to Okonkwo although in doing this he was very subtle. It was Okonkwo who broke the Week of Peace dedicated to the Earth-goddess, puffed up, Achebe implies, by pride of achievement — a sort of don't-care attitude — "like the little bird *Nza* who so forgot himself after a heavy meal that he challenged his *chi*." For this crime Okonkwo was punished by Ezeani. Killing Ikemefuna, Obierika tells Okonkwo, "will not please the Earth. It is the kind of action for which the goddess wipes out whole families." And to compound Okonkwo's crime against this goddess in the killing of Ikemefuna, we must remember that Ezeudu had warned Okonkwo: "That boy calls you father. Do not bear a hand in his death."

One could observe here that in many ways Ezeudu acts as the voice of reason in his relationship with Okonkwo who seems to display all the characteristics of the Freudian Id (it is after Ezeudu's death that all the misfortunes begin to crowd on Okonkwo). And between Okonkwo who seems to be unhappy in his sons (he kept till the end wishing Ezinma was a boy) and Ikemefuna, a special bond existed: Ikemefuna who never loved his paternal father had found in Okonkwo a satisfactory surrogate, and Okonkwo who was disappointed in Nwoye had "adopted" Ikemefuna as a son, allowing him the great privilege of carrying his bag for him — a privilege he seemed not to have extended to Nwoye. All this makes the murder of Ikemefuna all the more heinous.

Although the killing of Ikemefuna was very crudely handled by Achebe (one wonders why, as a victim for sacrifice he had to be killed or about to be killed from behind before he ran to Okonkwo who finally cut him down; why a group of seasoned men could not decoy a trusting stripling to the shrine and use the pot of wine he was carrying for libation before cutting him down, if not for the simple reason that Achebe bungled the scene to give Okonkwo responsibility for killing Ikemefuna in this melodramatic fashion), Okonkwo was convinced in himself that he had committed murder. He never felt the same long after this, and for the first time in his life he not only felt remorse but suffered physically for his crime. And as if to rub it in, Achebe uses animal imagery to describe Okonkwo. We are told that Okonkwo's "eyes were red and fierce like the eyes of a rat when it was caught by the tail and dashed against the floor"; that "he was so weak that his legs could hardly carry him. He felt like a drunken giant walking with the limbs of a mosquito." Even though he tried to rationalize his action, Okonkwo could not resolve his psychological conflict because Ikemefuna was not just another head, and his question, "How can a man who has killed five men in battle fall to pieces because he has added a boy to their number?" provided neither succour nor resolved the conflict.

In fact, after the death of Ikemefuna things began to go awry for Okonkwo. Obierika had told Okonkwo that *Ani* wipes out whole families for his crime. Unfortunately, the goddess widened the scope of its vengeance and involved the whole Clan. But first Okonkwo committed a "female" murder and had to go into exile while his friends return to destroy his property in vain hopes of cleansing the land. But Okonkwo returns and commits another murder — he kills the court messenger in cold blood, another crime against the Earth-goddess. And as if this was not enough, Okonkwo commits suicide thus committing in death a crime against *Ani* much worse than any other. As Obierika tells the Commissioner, to take Okonkwo's dangling body down is untenable:

> It is against our custom . . . it is an abomination for a man to take his own life. It is an offense against the Earth, and a man who commits it will not be buried by his clansmen. His body is evil, and only strangers may touch it.

Of course, in committing suicide Okonkwo displays another Igbo characteristic — a characteristic that slave traders discovered to their chagrin — that of resorting to suicide as a way out of difficulties in which every other alternative leads to personal humiliation and defeat. As the Haitians say, even today:

> *"Ibos pend' cor' a yo"* — the Igbos hang themselves.

It is common knowledge now that the tragedy of Okonkwo echoes a far greater one — that of the Clan whose living soul he is a manifestation. Here, again, the break-up of the Clan is not unmotivated. It comes as the aggregate of several telling strokes. I prefer to term it a series of *unmaskings*. The building of the Church in the Bad Bush which took no toll in lives unmasks the supposed potency of the Bad Bush as the repository of all the deadly elements in the clan; the intrusion of alien hands on the cult-slaves (the *Osu*) whose hair is shaven in contravention to native law and custom; the deliberate killing of the sacred python by a Christian; the shaving of the heads of titled men like Okonkwo in prison by such unhallowed hands as those of mere court-messengers (a rude travesty of the shaving of the *Osu* by Christian zealots); the unmasking of the *Egwugwu* by Christians — all these are desecrations of all that were held sacred and dignified in the clan. But the unmasking of the *Egwugwu* in itself revealed the powerlessness of the Clan Spirit and the triumph of alien forces, just as Okonkwo's suicide reveals his own powerlessness against the powers of the Commissioner.

Western critics speak patronizingly of Achebe's tremendous success in acquitting himself creditably in the novel genre which, they imply, is an "alien" African literary form, as if the novel form is a preserve of any race or culture. There is no doubt that eyebrows will be raised in Western critical circles when one labels *Things Fall Apart* an Igbo national Epic; after all, whoever heard of an African epic? But criticism thrives on certain demonstrable assumptions that have foundations in truth, not in treading the beaten track of palatable critical opinion.

BLACK AUTOBIOGRAPHY IN AFRICA AND AMERICA
by
JOSEPH BRUCHAC

    Autobiography has always been one of the most important of forms in black writing, both in Africa and in the Americas. And though there are often great differences between the life stories of such men as Richard Wright, whose tale of his childhood in the Delta south, *Black Boy,* has become an American classic since its publication in 1945 and Camara Laye, whose nostalgically idealized recounting of his youth in Guinea, *The Dark Child,* has also become a classic in its own right since its first publication in French under the title *L'Enfant Noir* in 1954. If we examine these works closely we are struck by the similarities between them — especially when we take note of the historical context which has produced them. Moreover, each book broadens our outlook on the other. But let us first look at the background.

    For the past five hundred years or so, the Western world and those nations and peoples unfortunate enough to be in a subservient relationship to it have been in an age of a very near-sighted and unusually color-conscious colonialism. We might mark the beginning of this period, as does John Henrik Clarke, at 1492, a year distinguished not so much by a bad Genoan navigator stumbling into the Caribbean islands of the New World while using maps made years before by Jewish traders, as by the marriage of Ferdinand and Isabella, an event which united Christian Spain and signalled the true end of a long and prosperous period of what we now must recognize as African colonialism. For several centuries, the dark Moors of North Africa had occupied large parts of Europe, bringing to the more ignorant natives such advances as mathematics and new ideas in medicine and architecture. Shakespeare's picture of Othello was drawn from the experience of his times, when Moorish emissaries were contacting Queen Elizabeth in the hopes of establishing an alliance with Britain which would allow them to reconquer Spain. Later writers than Shakespeare would not present a black character so straightforwardly again. As John Pepper Clark expressed it in his essay "The Legacy of Caliban" which appeared in the February, 1968 volume of *Black Orpheus:* "After Shakespeare, the treatment by English writers of the speech habits of the savage or black man becomes less original and imaginative, approaching (a) stereotype . . ."

We have lived in this age and perhaps it is unnecessary for me to spell out once more those characteristics of attitude which have made this age so tragic a one for the non-white. Perhaps, but then again, these characteristics are so much a part of our culture and our everyday lives that despite the work of men who have gone down to martyrdom in North America, in South Africa, in the Congo and elsewhere and despite the writings of those particular men I wish to focus on in this paper, these characteristics of a colonial age are to some degree still accepted, merely glossed over here and there by euphemisms.

The first of these characteristics is the assumption that the black man is bad because of the color of his skin, that his blackness is evil. The plantation owners of the ante-bellum South and the Boers of South Africa were not above using the Bible to justify both slavery and this view by referring to Noah's curse on Canaan in Genesis 9, 20-27. The reactions of contemporary law-enforcement officers in this country to the Black Panther Party may well have some connection with this deeply ingrained historical assumption in Western culture about blacks.

The second characteristic, which is closely linked to the first, is the assumption that black people in general, whether in America or Africa, are something less than human, are savages or the descendents of savages, unable to take care of themselves or run their own affairs without the benevolent guidance of a European. This assumption, like the first, neglects the wealth of African culture which existed before the disruptive coming of the Europeans to Africa. As the German Africanist, Jahnheinz Jahn, who is best known for his penetrating though somewhat over-simplified survey of neo-African culture *Muntu,* expresses it in the title of one of his books: *Wir Nennten Ihm Savagen* — "We Named Them Savages." The many arguments which are still heard in many quarters of government today about the inability of African nations to run their own affairs is only one example of this second characteristic assumption of Western culture.

These assumptions and others, of course, were quite convenient to justify the evils of slavery and colonialism. Not only were they believed in by the colonial master, but sometimes they were accepted by the enslaved or the colonized — not completely, for there have always been men like the Maroons of Jamaica, Toussaint L'Ouverture, Marcus Garvey, and W. E. B. DuBois, men who would see through the lie and pierce the veil. Phyllis Wheatley's poem "On Being Brought From Africa To America," though a plea for the humanity of the black, still looks at the Negro through a Western lens:

'Twas mercy brought me from my *Pagan* land,
Taught my benighted soul to understand
That there's a God, that there's a Saviour too:
Once I redemption neither sought nor knew.
Some view our race with scornful eye,
"Their color is a diabolic dye."
Remember, Christians, Negroes, black as Cain,
May be refined, and join th' angelic train.

Key words in this poem are "refined," "benighted" and "pagan." The phrase "Negroes, black as Cain" indicates that the poet was accepting the old idea of the implicit evil of black, and the entire major assumption of the poem seems to be not so much that Negroes are human as it is that Negroes can be made human if they are taught Christianity. Moreover, slavery is implicitly, for Phyllis Wheatley at least, a blessing in disguise.

Phyllis Wheatley, however, was a young girl when she was taken from Senegal and brought to America in 1761. Perhaps she had little memory of an Africa quite different from a benighted land of savage pageantry. It was the picture of a quite different Africa which would make the first major autobiography written by an African slave so unlike Phyllis Wheatley's writing in its portrayal of the dark mother. But then again, autobiography is by its very nature self-assertion, and the man who wrote in 1789 *The Interesting Narrative of Olaudah Equiano or Gustavus Vassa, The African* was a most unusual one.

Olaudah Equiano, born in 1745 in the kingdom of Benin, now a part of the present day nation of Nigeria, was kidnapped at the age of ten, through luck and perseverance was able to buy his way out of slavery, and became an active abolitionist and world traveller.

His words about his early days in Eboe, his home village include many such evocative passages as the following:

> We are almost a nation of dancers, musicians and poets. Thus every event such as a triumphant return from battle or other cause of public rejoicing is celebrated in public dances, which are accompanied with songs and music suited to the occasion.

and

> Agriculture is our chief employment, and everyone, even the women and children, are engaged in it. Thus we are all habituated to labour from our earliest years. Everyone contributes something to the common stock, and as we are unacquainted with idleness we have no beggars.

and

> As to religion, the natives believe that there is one Creator of all things.

The picture which begins to emerge, we hardly need stress, is quite different from one of benighted and ignorant savagery.

One of the most ironic parts of Equiano's autobiography, by the way, is his description of his emotions on being taken on board the slave ship. It illustrates both his sensitivity and that the role of savage was not, in this case, being played by black men:

> When I looked 'round the ship too, and saw a large furnace of copper boiling and a multitude of black people of every description chained together, every one of their countenances expressing dejection and sorrow, I no longer doubted my fate; and quite overpowered with horror and anguish, I fell motionless on the deck and fainted. When I recovered a little I found some black people about me. . . . I asked them if we were not to be eaten by those white men with horrible looks, red faces, and loose hair.

Olaudah Equiano's narrative marks the beginning of what was to be a long line of autobiographical works by African and Afro-American writers, all of which would have in common one great point — that they were written with a knowledge of the dehumanizing assumptions of Western culture about African and African-American peoples and that they would, in one way or another, endeavor to prove the falseness of these assumptions.

The black American equivalent of Olaudah Equiano was William Wells Brown, an unusually versatile man who was America's first real black man of letters. He later would write both plays and novels, including the famous book which Union soldiers carried with them into battle along with *Uncle Tom's Cabin*, *Clotelle, or,*

The President's Daughter, but it was in 1842 that his autobiography was published, ushering in an era of narratives, often partially written or at least edited by Abolitionists working with escaped slaves, which would present to the American public horrifying tales of bondage and escape. From 1840 to 1860 dozens of such book-length accounts were published, including, in 1845, the *Narrative of The Life of Frederick Douglass, An American Slave, Written By Himself.*

The number and the importance of the works of autobiographical nature written by Africans and African Americans since those first books by Brown and Equiano, make it impossible to go into them in any real depth at this time. One possible way of looking at them in terms of classification, however, might be of interest. It seems to me that we might be able to pick out three distinct patterns in terms of the autobiographical theme in Black writing: the Political Autobiography, the Personal and more Literary Autobiography, and the Autobiographical Novel.

The first on these is generally a work written by a person who is of considerable political importance. This, rather than the literary quality of the work (which may also be quite considerable) seems to be the main interest for the reader. Such works as Booker T. Washington's *Up From Slavery, The Autobiography of Malcolm X,* Chief Albert Luthuli's *Let My People Go,* and Kwame Nkrumah's *Ghana* are prominent examples of this type. So, too, are the celebrity biographies such as those of Dick Gregory, and Sammy Davis Jr.

The second is usually the work of a person whose first profession is writing. In many cases it states the experiences and themes which that writer has used in his other works. Generally, as a work of literature, it is more substantial and better written than the political autobiography. Wright's and Laye's books, as well as such books as Langston Hughes' *The Big Sea,* Ezekiel Mphalele's *Down Second Avenue* and *The Autobiography of W. E. B. DuBois* are examples of this second type.

(There is also a possible fourth category which seems to fit between these first two. It is the sentational autobiography, a work which may be a one-shot deal for its author and presents the writer as a sort of Ishmael character — though all black autobiographers are, in a sense, Ishmael. Prince Modupe's *I Was a Savage* and Claude Brown's *Manchild in the Promised Land* might be given as examples of this type.)

The last category, the Autobiographical Novel, is a work of fiction which either presents a character who is relating the story of his life or, in some way creates a character who is a mask of the author and lives the writer's own experience. James Weldon Johnson's *The Autobiography of An Ex-Colored Man* (which many people do not recognize as a work of fiction — Johnson's real autobiography, *Along This Way* was published in 1933, twenty-one years after the novel mistaken for his autobiography), Ayi Kwei Armah's powerful *Fragments,* Ferdinand Oyono's tragic *Boy* and even Ellison's *Invisible Man* might be placed in this category which, we find, includes a large percentage of all the writings done by African and Afro-American writers.

With these ideas in mind, let us now turn to those two major works which are, in a sense, the quintessence of the black autobiographical tradition.

At first glance, it might seem that apart from the similarity in their titles, *Black Boy* and *The Dark Child* have little in common. The first is a story of a childhood spent in the crushing poverty and inhuman brutality of a viciously color-conscious society. The second is almost a poem in its lyricism. It recounts in near-ideal terms the growing up in a strongly traditional society charged with principles of compassionate humanism of a boy who has none of the doubts about himself and his future which so haunted the young Richard Wright.

If we look again, however, we begin to see a similarity in pattern and motive between the two books.

Both Wright and Laye write of the forces which shape a man who, because he was born into a society and a time affected in one way or another by Western culture, must assert his own integrity against the dehumanizing assumptions of that society. *The Dark Child* was written while Laye was working in an automobile factory in France. Far behind him was the childhood which is so vividly described in his book. He was a member of the working class of France, France the great mother of art and culture, yet like the poets of negritude he was not satisfied with being a black Frenchman. He knew that he never could be that, partially because of the elitist nature of the French policies of assimilation, partially because his own cultural heritage was so rich and so true. To find himself, to define himself to both the Western world and himself he returned to childhood. His story does not begin when he was rescued from the savagery of a primitive Africa and it does not end with his becoming an honored citizen of France. It is not a success story, and though it may seem charged with happiness and satisfaction when compared to the agonies of the Delta South Wright pictures, one of the most real elements of *The Dark Child* is a sense of loss. It begins:

> I was a little boy playing around my father's hut. How old would I have been at that time? I can not remember exactly. I must have been very young: five, maybe six years old. My mother was in the workshop with my father, and I could just hear their familiar voices above the noise of the anvil and the conversation of the customers.

After this picture of a secure world, surrounded by the presence and voices of family and friends, the agony of the last few pages of the book is much clearer. Because of his success in trade school Laye is to go to France. It is the dark child's mother who reacts the strongest to his forthcoming departure, knowing full well that more than mere miles will separate them:

> "Am I never to have peace. Yesterday it was the school in Conarky; today it's the school in France; tomorrow . . . what will it be tomorrow? Every day there's some mad scheme to take my son from me. . . . Have you already forgotten how sick he was in Conarky? But that's not enough for you. Now you want to send him to France. . . . What are they thinking about at the school. Do they imagine I'm going to live my whole life apart from my son? Die with him far away? Have they no mothers, those people? They can't have. They wouldn't have gone so far away from home if they had."

To be sure, the contrast is very real with Richard Wright's separation from his family. When Richard Wright headed north, he was not leaving a world of security and order. In fact, his family wished to flee with him:

> The accidental visit of Aunt Maggie to Memphis formed a practical basis for my planning to go north. . . . My mother, Aunt Maggie, my brother and I held long conferences, speculating on the prospects of jobs and the cost of apartments in Chicago. And every time we conferred, we defeated ourselves. It was impossible for all four of us to go at once; we did not have enough money.

But both Wright and Laye are heading into the unknown, forced to leave the life which has formed them by pressures from outside, pressures exerted by Western culture. When Laye ends his story with these words:

> Later on I felt something hard when I put my hand in my pocket. It was the map of the *metro*. . . .

We should not have to stretch our imagination too far to realize that in a very real sense he is about to enter the metro, the subway, the underground world of white civilization, to descend into hell. And from Wright's other books, we should be able to see clearly that what awaited the young Richard in the cities of the north was also far from a promised land.

There are other facets of these two books in addition to their concluding flights to centers of Western civilization which can be meaningfully compared. One of these areas is education.

Both books, dealing with the coming of age of a young man, center on the education which is a major aspect of that maturity. Where Richard Wright's formal education is haphazard and often capricious, as in the case of his experiences as a pupil of his Aunt Addie's in religious school, Laye's is planned and structured. Yet it is structured in such a way as to draw him inevitably further from his own heritage, as his mother so wisely sees. The formal education of each of the young protagonists, however, is not so important as another kind of education having to do with society. And it is at this point that we see the greatest contrast between the lives of Wright and Laye. Wright is taught, by beatings from his family, by painful example, and by the often threatening attitudes of his white employers that he must not aspire to rise above his place in the Jim Crow South. When he refuses to read the valedictory speech written by his 9th grade principal instead of his own he is well on his way to a final rejection of that society.

Laye, on the other hand, is taught in the meaningful rituals of manhood and circumcisions what it is to be a man in an ordered and humane African society. His ritual of passage is one of acceptance.

Another area which is important in both books is that of family. There are obvious differences. Richard Wright's family is fatherless and most of his descriptions of family life seem to focus on the terrible conflicts he had with mother, grandmother, and various aunts and uncles. In *The Dark Child* we see a closely knit family with a father and mother both of whom are not only figures of pride to the young Laye, but even figures of magic. His father has a guardian spirit in the form of a small black snake which visits him at his forge. His mother is familiar with all of the mysteries of his country and has mysterious powers. To say, however, that Wright's family cared less for their child than did Laye's seems to me to be a misinterpretation. Their actions to chasten the indomitable spirit of a very proud and extremely sensitive youth were actions taken to save him from the lynching which was usually the regard for the sort of individuality he was showing. It is in council with his relatives and with their very direct help that Wright makes the decision to leave the Delta. Even further, if we note the closeness of uncles, aunts, cousins and so on to Wright's immediate family, we realize that we are witnessing the American equivalent, even after years of slavery and degradation, of the African extended family.

Ralph Ellison, in an essay on *Black Boy* has called Wright's autobiography blues, defining the blues as:

> an impulse to keep the painful details and episodes of a brutal experience alive in one's aching consciousness, to finger its jagged grain, and to transcend it, not by the consolation of philosophy but by squeezing from it a near-tragic, near-comic lyricism.

We can hear this blues note in the passages when Wright finds himself wakening to the mystery and beauty of the ambiguous world around him:

> The days and hours began to speak now with a clearer tongue. Each experience had a sharp meaning of its own.
> There was the breathless anxious fun of chasing and catching flitting fireflies on drowsy summer nights. . . .
> There was the excitement of fishing in muddy county creeks with my grandpa on cloudy days. . . .
> There was the fear and awe I felt when Grandpa took me to a sawmill to watch the giant whirring steel blades whine and scream as they bit into wet green logs. . . .

And we hear it most clearly of all in the last paragraphs of the book when Wright says:

> Yet, deep down, I knew that I could never really leave the South. . . . I was taking a part of the South to transplant in alien soil, to see if it could grow differently, if it could drink of new and cool rains, bend in strange winds, respond to the warmth of other suns, and perhaps, to bloom. . . . And if that miracle ever happened, then I would know that there was yet hope in that southern swamp of despair and violence, that light would emerge even out of the blackness of the southern night.

If Wright's *Black Boy* is the blues, then Camara Laye's *The Dark Child* is the music of the praise singer, the muted balafong and drum, a music which may be soft yet is as strong and deep as the beat of the human heart.

Both blues and praise song are African forms, and as a symbol of the strength of human dignity Africa lives in the writing of both Laye and Wright. Wright's Africa is deep within himself, it is the tough strength of a persevering descendent of African slaves. Laye's is the Africa his incomplete Europeanization has drawn him away from. And in reading their works and the books of other African and Afro-American autobiographers, we see that it is that Africa of human compassion and dignity to which we must all return.

BLACK AMERICAN POETRY, ITS LANGUAGE, AND THE FOLK TRADITION

by

Alvin Aubert

A consideration of the language of Afro-American poetry, past or present, begins with an acknowledgement of the essential relationship of Afro-American poetry to, first, black cultural *evolution*, and second, that evolution's acceleration, the black cultural revolution of the 1950's onward. By black cultural evolution I mean the cultural counterpart of the agonizing process, from slavery to the 1950s, which marks the Afro-American's long, slow, and painful re-emergence into history from an initial condition of violently enforced non-history and consequential non-being. By black cultural revolution I mean the cultural counterpart of the accelerated pace of that re-emergence which dates from the 1950s.

Our concern here is historical perspective, in particular the value of a sense of continuity regarding the Afro-American experience. We should see clearly that just as in the political realm such phenomena as black nationalism and militant protest did not begin in the years since 1956, the characteristic features of Afro-American poetry did not spring into being in recent decades. We should also begin to see that the issue is essentially one of the relationship of the poet and his public: in terms of Afro-American, the black poet and the black community.

A living art requires something of a unified collective sensibility, a common field of creative activity and formative appreciation. Such a field could eventuate, under the appropriate conditions, in a new aesthetic. It is unique of Afro-American culture that of the several sub-cultures in this country, it alone provides the conditions for achieving such a sensibility, and the consequent feasibility of an aesthetic — a black aesthetic expressive of a mutually formative relationship between the black community and the black artist. W.E.B. DuBois was one of the early sensors of this inherent quality of Afro-American life. It informs his brief but highly seminal observations in *The Souls of Black Folk* on the need for a more positive relationship between the Afro-American artist and his community. He notes that "the innate love of harmony and beauty that set the ruder souls of his people a-dancing and a-singing raised but confusion and doubt in the soul of the black artist; for the beauty revealed to him was the soul-beauty of a race which his larger audience [whites and befuddled ne-groes] despised, and he could not articulate the message of another people."[1]

Alain Locke, too, touches the heart of the matter when in his 1925 essay on the spirituals he reminds us of the communal nature of these songs, observing that they "are essentially congregational, not theatrical, just as they are essentially a choral not a solo form."[2] Note also in this regard James Weldon Johnson's judgement, in *The Book of American Negro Poetry*, that the best poems of such poets of the 20s as Langston Hughes, Sterling Brown, Frank Horne, Arna Bontemps, and Waring Cuney are those that spring from "race consciousness."[3]

The quality that bespeaks a potential for a black aesthetic is evident in the best works in all fields of artistic endeavor in Afro-America. We in fact recognize it, in time, as coterminous with the formative vital force, or *essential rhythm,* of Afro-American life and art. It is a matter of prime concern among those in the contemporary Black Arts Movement, the pre-eminent figure in which remains Imamu Amiri Baraka (LeRoi Jones), first among Afro-American poets to project a positive, uncompromising vision of the corporate blackness of Afro-America. "The whole race connected in its darkness, in its sweetness,"[4] Baraka declares, figuring forth a Black Humanism the purveyor of which is the black artist, and which in turn forms the value basis of the emergent black aesthetic.

The essential rhythm of Afro-American life manifests itself most clearly in language. It emanates from the urgency to communicate, to "move" — to "affect," to employ a more current critical term. Rooted in the pain of bondage and in the circumstantially burdensome love of freedom, this affective urgency is the hallmark of Afro-American art, from the "Sorrow Songs" of slavery to the poems of the most contemporary Afro-American poets. Its aim is not so much a call to action as a summons to unification, prerequisite to meaningful action. For the foremost need of black Being in this country remains the crucial one of relation, of community for survival. Such a community is to be founded on positive values, for the most part on newly articulated values based in black life in terms of the *reality* of the black experience. Hence, a Black Humanism, as Don L. Lee, a disciple of Baraka, expresses it:

create *man* blackman . . .
walk thru the
world
as if You are world itself,[5]

The earliest reservoir of the essential rhythm we speak of here is of course the rather extensive body of Afro-American folk creations: spirituals, sermons, prayers; work songs, tales, and legends; and the blues and jazz. Sophisticated black writers of the turn of the century were in effect charged with the task of negotiating an adjustment between the "folk" and the "literary" in terms of their work. It was their obligation, in Ralph Ellison's words, "to explore the full range of American humanity and to affirm those quailties which are of value." These writers soon recognized the folk forms as prototypes of black art, an abundant source from which to infuse their lettered creations with the essential rhythm. Even the enigmatic Paul Lawrence Dunbar was aware of this burden of adjustment, however misguided his recourse to the artificial "negro" dialect of the white-blackface minstrel tradition, and to the unrealistic social and economic philosophies that Darwin T. Turner attributes to him.[6]

It remained for James Weldon Johnson to provide a corrective to Dunbar and his imitators, and in so doing point a new direction for Afro-American poetry. Johnson clearly recognized one aspect of the limitation of dialect, its defect by association with the parodic minstrel tradition. Johnson must have sensed, too, its inability *alone* to rise above the level of mere orthographic speech notation, to render the essential rhythm of Afro-American life. The dialect used by Sterling A. Brown, for example, superior to Dunbar's as it is, would be of small consequence without the essential rhythm underlying his poems in the folk vein. Indeed, most of Brown's poems in that vein could easily forego the use of dialect, as a number of them in effect do. The following stanza from Brown's poem "Sister Lou" provides an example of the superfluity of dialect, as well as the sufficiency of syntax and rhythm to convey a sense of the Afro-American ethos, its essential rhythm:

> Jesus will find yo' bed fo' you
> Won't no servant evah bother wid yo' room.
> Jesus will lead you
> To a room wid windows
> Openin' on cherry trees an' plum trees
> Bloomin' everlastin'.[7]

The double negative and peculiar inversion of the second line are particular cases in point. Unless my ear betrays me, the idea it expresses could hardly have been uttered in quite this way by anyone outside the black community. It is the polarizing line of the stanza, and it achieves its effect irrespective of the dialect orthography.

James Weldon Johnson seems to have recognized also, that the artistic embodiment of the essential rhythm of black life requires as a model, not the everyday speech of the black community but that speech stylistically *formed* to the uses of folk art. In his poems in *God's Trombones,* which grew from the poet's memories of the performances of "the old-time Negro preacher," Johnson captures the essential rhythm of black life. He does not attempt a duplication of the folk rhythm, but plays the rhythm of the poems contrapuntally against the remembered cadences of his folk source. The first poem in the book, "The Creation," begins:

> And God stepped out on space,
> And he looked around and said:
> I'm lonely —
> I'll make me a world.[8]

The atuned ear catches in these lines not only the rhythm of the folk sermon, but of the gospel and jazz beat as well. In "The Prodigal Son," we get the following passage, reflective of the stacatto pointing, for want of a better term, which places the folk sermon in the traditional call and response pattern of African origin, designed in the sermon to elicit highly charged affirmations from the congregation, usually "amens," but sometime just "yes!", as extrapolated in parenthesis.

> Then the young man came to himself —   (Yes!)
> He came to himself and said:
> In my father's house are many mansions,   (Yes!)
> Ev'ry servant in his house has bread to eat,   (Yes!)
> Ev'ry servant in his house has a place to sleep; (Amen!)
> I will arise and go to my father.[9]   (O, yes!)

The mode of memory involved in Johnson's use of his folk sources is not that of the mind alone, but of the blood and bone as well, if not primarily of the blood and bone. Also, the poems lend themselves to various modes of appreciation, from the neo-folk to the most sophisticated, and they work nearly as well on the page as when carried by the voice.

The practice we have noted in Johnson continues in Langston Hughes, although in a somewhat more secular vein, mainly through the use of what Hughes refers to as "the Negro folk-song forms" — the spirituals, the blues, and jazz. In another context Hughes speaks of the influence on his poetic sensibility of the songs he heard in the "barrel houses and shouting churches" on Seventh Street, Washington, D. C. These songs, Hughes says, have "the pulse beat of the people who kept on going," who endured. Of black music in general, Hughes has this to say:

> Like the waves of the sea coming one after another, always one after another, like the earth moving around the sun, night, day — night, day — night, day — forever, so is the undertow of black music with its rhythm that never betrays you, its strength like the beat of the human heart, its humor, and its rooted power.[10]

Hughes' best poems in the blues mode are those which achieve an approximation of the blues form and rhythm rather than a more or less exact replication of these qualities. As in the case of his best jazz oriented poems, the result is more effective when, as we read the poem, rememberd rhythms of musical performances are activated in a corner of the mind — not in the sense of accompaniment, but of a paradigmatic set of references. Perhaps more so than James Weldon Johnson, Langston Hughes provides a model study of the assimilation of folk art forms to the uses of sophisticated modes of expression.

With these distinctions in mind, compare the two passages that follow, the first from Hughes' poem "Morning After" and the second from "Reverie on the Harlem River". Note the following elements in the first passage: (1) the traditional blues pattern of "statement" (lines 1-4) and "response" (lines 5-6); (2) the characteristic repetition with slight variation in the "statement"; (3) the "answer" to the statement that the response gives, (4) the rhyme scheme, (5) length of the line, and (6) the achievement of a syncopated effect by the placement of the pronoun "I" at the end of lines one and three, and "that" at the end of line five. Note also, in comparing the two stanzas, the reliance more on accent than on the traditional Western metrical scheme, allowing for greater rythmical complexity and underscoring what Janheinz Jahn refers to as "the specifically Negro or African rhythmic element," allowing for "a more or less indefinite number of unaccented syllables . . .

between stresses."[11] Comparatively, lines 1 and 2 of both stanzas are of approximately equal rhythmical value despite the difference in line length. Also, observe in the second passage the abandonment, in stanzaic terms, of the circular pattern of "statement" and "response," in favor of a more strictly linear progression, but only to assimilate the circular in terms of the structure of the poem as a whole. In "Reverie on the Harlem River" the first two stanzas correspond structurally to the repeated, slightly varied "statement" (as in the first passage quoted), and the third (final) stanza has as its structural counterpart the "response".

I. I was so sick last night I
Didn't hardly know my mind.
So sick last night I
Didn't know my mind.
I drunk some bad licker that
Almost made me blind.

II. Did you ever go down to the river —
Two a.m. midnight by your self?
Sit down by the river
And wonder what you got left?[12]

The labor of the turn-of-the-century Afro-American poet to shape his poem to the rhythmical form of essential Afro-American life was of short duration. We may read an account of its demise in terms of James H. Emanuel's historical sketch tracing the emergence of the new black consciousness among intellectuals of the 1960s. The sketch begins with the death of "the bold black artist" who in the 1920s was being crowned "the New Negro." This new creature "slowly died," says Emanuel. "In the 1930s, the Depression emaciated him. In the 1940s, global warfare drained the energies and diverted the attitudes vital to his recovery. In the 1950s, fitful surges toward racial integration deluded him into believing that the question of his death had become less relevant. When the 1960s began, his grandchildren waved a respectful but apprehensive farewell from their fiery buses and grim lunch counters in the South. On the verge of the 1970's, they threw away his clothes, his hair, and his name. They emerged as the Young Blacks, fevered by the past and determined to make non-negotiable demands upon the future."[13]

The counter-transformation of the 40s and 50s depicted by Emanuel has its counterpart in the integrationist/assimilationist impulse among black poets during that period. (The exception is Langston Hughes, a steady center of allegiance to the essential rhythm of black life, a constant fire from whose flame the young poets of the 50s and 60s were to kindle their torches.) Generally, the sensibility of Afro-American poets seemed caught in the pallid clutches of the New Criticism, the retreat from man, transfixed by what Imamu Amiri Baraka calls "the deathly grip of the white eye." White critical praise was admittedly the main source of praise or blame during these years of almost complete critical silence on the part of black intellectuals, but white praise was accorded the black poet — the black writer in general — in proportion to the black writer's willing obliteration of his blackness, usually by "aesthetically" transcending its "inherent ugliness," or by rising above its concreteness to the realm of the abstract universal. Accommodation, if not conformity, seemed on the verge of becoming the order of the day. This is evident, for example, in much of the poetry of Melvin B. Tolson, Robert Hayden, Owen Dodson, and the early Gwendolyn Brooks. I do not intend an indictment of these poets. It is not that they forsook their socio-political obligations to the fact of their blackness. But lured by the "mermaids singing each to each" within the fancied security of the white literary establishment, they went in danger of obscuring the essential linkage between *their black selves* and the Afro-American community, to the detriment of both. Gwendolyn Brooks discusses this aspect of her writing career in an interview which appears in the April 1971 issue of *Essence* magazine:

> In the 1950s and early 1960s, I was still a loner, I had a few black friends and a few white friends. I would go to their homes, they would come to my house, and that was about the extent of my meaningful social relationships. I used to give great big literary parties, too, cramping more than a hundred people into this house ... I thought I was happy, and I saw myself going on like that the rest of my days. I thought it was the way to live. I wrote, these people wrote, we saw each other, we talked about writing. But it was white writing, the different trends among the whites. Today I am conscious of the fact that — my people are black people; it is to them that I appeal for understanding.

We praise the technical mastery of Melvin B. Tolson's two major works, *Libretto for the Republic of Liberia* and *Harlem Gallery*, but is not technical mastery a relative matter? At any rate, the technical mastery sorely needed in the black arts remains one that is reflective of a vitally communicative, mutually formative relationship between the black artist and his community.

Earlier Afro-American poets achieved the beginning of such a relationship. They did it, as we have indicated, by tapping the rich body of Afro-American folk art for the essence of black life, particularly as that essence inheres in language. Contemporary Afro-American poets who endorse the validity and feasibility of a black aesthetic are determined to continue the movement, relatively dormant during the 1940s and 50s, to re-establish contact between the black artist and his community. They aim at drawing the black community into an active role in the arts. They envision as a distinct possibility a mutually formative creative relationship between artist and community. They hope to issue into being a common field of artistic creation and appreciation, and a black aesthetic, rooted in black life, past and present.

Any study of this aspect of the Black Arts Movement would include the later poems (and other works) of Imamu Amiri Baraka. It would include just about all the poets in the anthology *Black Fire,* edited by Baraka (as LeRoi Jones) and Larry Neal. Among the poems in the book are numerous evocative of spirituals, gospel songs, and folk sermons; of the blues and jazz; and of just plain rappin' and finger-poppin'. In these poems, the folk basis of Afro-American art is affirmed, not only through stylistics, but in terms of imagery and theme as well. Regard in this respect Larry Neal's poem "Malcolm X — An Autobiography," in *Black Fire.* The following passage from Neal's poem represents the persona, Malcolm, at one stage of his growing awareness of the essential meaning of black life. The setting is a microcosmic Harlem. The passage itself is mildly evocative of folk rhythms:

> But there is rhythm here. Its own special substance:
> I hear Billie sing, no good man, and dig Prez, wearing
>   the Zoot
> suit of life — the porkpie hat tilted at the correct angle.
> through the Harlem smoke of beer and whisky, I understand the
> mystery of the signifying monkey.

Imamu Amiri Baraka in "Sermon for Our Maturity," employs the rhythm and rhetoric of the folk sermon. The following passage should be regarded in the context of our earlier comments on the passage from James Weldon Johnson's "The Creation." The "uh" at the end of the fifth and tenth lines achieves the effect of the folk preacher's breath-punctuation, as well as that of the "statement" and "response" pattern of African origin (the parenthesised "yes!" of lines 13-15 are extrapolated.):

> Your relationship with all the things
> the seen
> and the un seen
> the felt
> and the need to be felt   uh

```
            ray
                touch me
        touched pulled thru ether
        speed eater space lover
you need to get better        uh
you need to experience better times Negro
We love you negro Love you betta
if you got betta        (Yes!)
Love yrself betta       (Yes!)
If you got betta        (Yes!)
```

The poem from which this is taken appears in the Winter-Spring 1970 issue of *Journal of Black Poetry,* most of the poems in which reflect some aspect of the Afro-American folk sources.

Don L. Lee in "Blackman/an unfinished history" (from his book *We Walk the Way of the New World*) combines the imagery of photo technology and the rhythm of black music (jazz) to achieve an interesting effect. He exhorts the black man:

```
be a New World picture.    click,    click.
blackman click blackman click into tomorrow.
Spaced from the old thoughts into
the new. Zooomm.  Zoooommmmm    Zooommmmmm.
click.
design yr own neighborhood, Zoom,              it can be,
teach yr own children,   Zoom   Zoom           it can be,
build yr own loop,   Zoom   Zoom               it can be,
Watch out world greatness is coming.   click.      click.
```

As a final note, a great deal of the new black poetry is in the oratorical mode — poems for the voice more so than for the page. This is not surprising, given the high vocality of black life at its liveliest; the high regard for the spoken word; the living in and through language when language was all the world the black man had to move around in, to inhabit; and the oratorical cast of Afro-American folk art. In the final analysis, it is a matter of what voice does to language. It is essential, therefore, to hear some of these poems read (rendered is perhaps the more accurate term) and preferably by the poets themselves.

FOOTNOTES

1. *The Souls of Black Folk* (Greenwich, Conn., 1961), p. 18. The problem takes on wider meaning in terms of DuBois' concept of "double-consciousness" which, when applied to the black artist, assumes a form answerable to the term triple-consciousness.
2. "The Negro Spirituals," in *The New Negro* (New York, 1969), p. 202. An Atheneum Press re-issue.

3. *The Book of American Negro Poetry* (New York, 1921, 1931, 1959), p. 220.
4. *Black Magic Poetry* (New York, 1969), p. (ii). For more of Baraka on Black Humanism, see his articles in recent issues of *Black World* (formerly *Negro Digest*), *Journal of Black Poetry*, and *The Black Scholar*.
5. *We Walk the Way of the New World* (Detroit, 1970), p. 33.
6. "Paul Lawrence Dunbar: the Rejected Symbol," *The Journal of Negro History*, LII (January, 1967), 1-13.
7. Abraham Chapman, ed., *Black Voices* (New York, 1968), p. 405.
8. *God's Trombones* (New York, 1969), p. 17. A Viking Press re-issue.
9. *Ibid.*, p. 24.
10. *The Big Sea* (New York, 1963), p. 209.
11. *Neo-African Literature* (New York, 1969), p. 167.
12. *Selected Poems of Langston Hughes* (New York, 1969), pp. 42-43.
13. "Blackness Can: A Quest for Aesthetics," in Addison Gayle, Jr., ed., *The Black Aesthetic* (New York, 1971), pp. 192-193.

RICHARD WRIGHT: THE EXPATRIATE PATTERN
by
PAUL C. SHERR

The fictional writings of Richard Wright have caused critics, scholars, journalists and graduate students to attribute his success or failure to the influence of James T. Farrell, Gertrude Stein, John Dos Passos, F. Scott Fitzgerald, Sherwood Anderson, Theodore Dreiser and others. They have labeled him a naturalist, a freudian, and an existentialist. One scholar proposed that he was white. These people came to such conclusions, we assume, in an effort to better understand Richard Wright and to place him in the spectrum of American literature. It is within the spectrum of American literature and the American experience that I wish to consider the novels of Richard Wright written while he was an expatriate as a means to darken the curriculum.

Viewed in a kindly light, an expatriate is one who leaves his native land because he believes that his homeland is in some way or another unaesthetic, gross, repressive, or unappreciative of him. The image of the immigrant from Europe to America as pictured in the history books is that of the common man, finally afforded a way out of poverty, repression and inequality, into a land of milk and honey, of opportunity for everyone. Students of American literature, however, know that almost immediately after the founding of the United States in 1789, strong feelings of disenchantment with America arose in the hearts of 19th century American men of letters. Irving, Cooper, Emerson, Hawthorne, Howells, James, and Frederic found America distasteful for a variety of reasons: Americans had few or no manners, America had no heritage which could supply material about which to write, America could not accept the literary products of her own writers, Americans were anti-intellectual, Americans were unaesthetic, being too preoccupied with material matters to establish a climate conducive to the production of literature and art. And so the exodus from "Utopia." Instead of going west, almost to a man, our 19th century literary leaders returned to Europe where, they believed, a climate existed sensitive to the needs of the creative spirit, where an educated, aesthetic elite welcomed and enthusiastically supported and understood what the creative artist proposed to contribute to the total well-being of man. This reversal of direction is at first reckoning contradictory, but by acknowledging the strong human impulse to record events, to use history as a guide for the present, to lay claim to a heritage as sufficient cause for membership in the "club," we have little difficulty understanding why Americans want to go home again, to Europe.

For most American whites, family ties run to Europe, Western and Eastern. What attracts us are the stories about our families, about the towns they came from, the pictures in a family album plus a historical and literary heritage that tells us about Westminster Cathedral, about Rome, the Caesars, the Church and the popes, about the Oktoberfest, Rasputin, pornography in Denmark, Oh, la, la in France, and a bottle of Sack and a glass of Madeira, my dear. What does the average American do when he can't stand himself and his way of life? He runs. He's either "On the Road" with Jack Kerouac, down the Mississippi with Huck Finn, "Up, Up and Away" with the Fifth Dimension, seeking "Our Old Home" with Nathaniel Hawthorne, trying to horn in on genteel Europe with Henry James, fighting a civil war or hunting lions with Hemingway, or for the bourgeoisie simply dashing along a highway at 80 miles an hour at two o'clock in the morning in a Jaguar, Ferrari or Porsche. All of us are Expatriates in spirit if not in deed.

From the beginning of our literary expatriation, most of the expatriates came from the Eastern seaboard: Irving, Cooper, Hawthorne, Henry James, Edith Wharton, Harold Frederic. The pattern was broken in the 19th century by William Dean Howells, a midwesterner. As the literary spawning place moved west, the source of American expatriates moved west, including specifically that group of famous ones we associate with the 1920's: Hemingway, Fitzgerald, T. S. Eliot, Sinclair Lewis, Ezra Pound, and by extension Richard Wright. With each of these men, there was a move to the East, either to Chicago and then on to Europe. Like the hero of Richard Wright's *The Long Dream* who starts in the South, heads north to New York and at novel's end, leaves for Paris, Richard Wright started in the southern part of the mid-west, Mississippi, moved to Chicago, then to New York, and ultimately, complete expatriation in Paris. Wright and his hero follow a pattern that is totally American, black and white: dissatisfaction with the place of birth, the move to the big city and its impersonal way of life, and the final break with the United States into a foreign country, most frequently, somewhere in Europe.

In a limited sense, expatriation (out of country) implies physical removal. In a broader sense, it is removal or escape or withdrawal from whatever is undesirable or unpleasant, generated by the interplay of personality and society. The penchant for Americans to move on, looking for freedom, was first called attention to by Crevecoeur; later, by Frederick Jackson Turner. It is within both purviews that I wish to consider Richard Wright in the expatriate pattern: first, as an American citizen and an American literary artist returning to the heritage of Europe, specifically to France which for the 1920's generation of expatriates stood for fundamental freedoms, secondly, as a writer of fiction in whose works, the American syndrome of running away from social, political, or psychological pressures is presented in the guise of heroes who are black and white but unalterably American.

The expatriates of the 1920's differ in many ways from those of the 19th century. Not only did they come from the mid-west but also they were symptomatic of any American phenomenon that came about as the result of World War I: for the first time in the history of the United States, vast numbers of Americans of all classes travelled abroad, learning about the mores not only of other cultures, but specifically the cultures of their forebears. The expatriates of the 1920's returned to Europe because they had learned during the war that one could live there more cheaply, that there were things to do, things to see that one could not do or see at home, that one could choose to do absolutely nothing but live in Europe without feeling terribly guilty, that people there tolerated diverse political, social and theological views, and above all, that a hedonistic attitude toward living prevailed. In short, to quote Gertrude Stein, "France was friendly, and it let you along."[1]

Gertrude Stein was one of the major reasons why America's literati of the Teens and Twenties went to Europe. To know her, to be invited by her was an indication that one had a position on the ladder of success. To Richard Wright, Gertrude Stein's recognition of him was of an extremely personal nature, writing to him:

"Dear Richard, it is obvious that you and I are the only two geniuses of this area."[2] She personally met him when he arrived in Paris early in the spring of 1946, a trip he made in response to an invitation from the French Government.

Richard's first sojourn in Paris was brief. From such first emotional expressions as "For the first time in my life, I stepped on free soil," or "I'm at last in Paris, city of my dreams. . . . Will I ever be myself again after all this?",[3] he began to despair after six months. He could not adjust to the tempo of French life, for he found that he was doing no work. He returned to New York, experienced a series of extremely unpleasant situations in Greenwich Village, and returned to Paris in 1947, remaining in France, with the exception of various trips, until his death in 1960.

It was not a trouble-free expatriation. Although he had the friendship of Gide, Sartre, Simone De Beauvoir, Carson MacCullers, and others, he could not escape the anguish that came to him when his suspicions arose that people, French people, white people, black people were out to get him, his family, his Siamese cat, his huge Oldsmobile, and mostly, his time for writing, that is, his very life.[4]

Whatever his personal difficulties, including serious attempts at understanding the confusions of French politics, at the exploitation of white peasants and lower classes in Italy and Spain, Wright decided to remain an expatriate because he faced fewer difficulties living in France as a black man, than he had in the U.S.A. Excluding his personal problems with his self image, Richard Wright went to France for the same reasons that the expatriates of the 1920's went there, and he remained there because he found what they were looking for; as Gertrude Stein put it: "France was friendly, and it let you alone."

Wright's works of fiction, written during his period of expatriation, contain elements that suggest that he was in part preoccupied with the importance of physical removal from point of stress. The pattern of physical removal from the South to the North to large city, East to New York, and plans for actual expatriation to Paris appears in part or whole in all three of his novels written after 1947: *The Outsider* (1953), *Savage Holiday* (1954), and *The Long Dream* (1957).

At the core of the expatriate pattern are the twin seeds of discontent and of free will to run from frustration. Denied the freedom to move, the expatriate ceases to exist, except in fantasy. Neither Richard Wright, nor his heroes, exist as anything other than human beings, facing real problems in the real world of the United States. The dilemma of Cross Tamon, the hero of *The Outsider*, is immediately identifiable. He is an unhappy, frustrated man, wanting out of a way of life which he feels has denied him his freedom. He despises his job, hates his wife, and resents his mother who constantly reminds him that he is something less than a responsible human being. His friends chide him with friendly admiration about his "Quadruple A Program:" "Alcohol, Abortion, Alimony and Automobiles", the first of which has played hell with his liver. Damon considers his anti-social acts to be manifestations of his free will, his control over his world, or to use his own words "that was the . . . time [I] felt like God . . ." When? When he tossed money out of the window of an office building so that he could watch "the commotion of all them little ant-like folks down there going wild, scrambling and scratching and clawing after them few pieces of money . . ."[5] Or on another occasion when cynically playing Santa Claus, he sent all his friends a subscription to a magazine, using the gift order forms published in the magazines, but signing the names of the people to whom he sent the subscriptions rather than his own. "Man the whole South Side was in a dither that Christmas morning. Folks was thanking other folks for presents the other folks didn't know nothing about. And Crossy was listening and watching and saying nothing."[6]

Cross Damon, with his mother, came out of the South to the North, to Chicago. His frustrations, at moments appeased by alcohol or by playing God, drove him to other desperate measures: abandoning his wife and children, committing adultery and deliberate murder. Even when his erratic behavior backed him into a corner, he could admit that he had placed himself into that position by his own free will: "He was properly trapped. There was nothing more to say. This was a cold and vindictive Gladys created by him."[7] Oddly, Cross Damon does not exercise his free will by running away; rather, when he is mistaken for another black man who is killed and maimed beyond recognition in a subway accident, Damon allows his world to believe that he is the dead man. Then Cross Damon is free to start afresh, which he does. How? "He ordered a beer . . . wondering who he would be for the next four or five days, until he left for, say, New York. To begin his new life . . . he would be a Negro who had just come up fresh from the Deep South . . ."[8]

Cross Damon's misuse of his free will mixed with fate takes him to New York where, like Richard Wright, he falls in love with a white girl. Like Richard Wright, her concept of freedom is associated with France, specifically Paris. Her enthusiasm sounds quite like Wright's own ebullience when he first arrived in Paris: "She spoke . . . of her love of music, poetry, and the beauty of France, which she had seen last summer." Her entries in her diary reflect the same enthusiasm: "I'm at last in Paris, city of my dreams . . . the beauty of this wonderful Paris . . . The art exhibits, the artists' studies, the sense of leisure, the love of beauty — will I ever be myself again after all this?" Like Richard, she is enthralled by Notre Dame, by twilight and dawn, the quietness of the city, the intensity of the feelings generated by the political factions.[9]

In New York, Cross Damon murders people and loses a complicated game of intrigue as he pits his intelligence and his philosophy of life against the combined intelligence of the Communist party. Cross loses. The Party murders him. What is of interest here is the result of Cross Damon's decision to play God. In Chicago, his pranks gain him the guarded admiration of his peers. In New York, his lashing out against the forces which seek to prevent his practicing free will destroys him. The nineteenth century American expatriates did not destroy themselves by lashing out at forces which they thought stifled them. They fled. Cross Damon does not become an expatriate. He fights and dies. Interestingly, Richard Wright asserts that the death of Cross Damon is directly due to his personal shortcomings, shortcomings which are precisely those which the 19th century literary artists accused the United States of: "For Cross had had no party, no myths, no tradition, no race, no soil, no culture and no ideas . . ."[10] What the United States lacked for the 19th century expatriates, life lacked for Cross Damon. Unlike Richard Wright and the 19th century expatriates who escaped from the United States, Cross Damon could not escape from himself by his carefully organized plan to play God. The society he tries to control does him in. Expatriate Richard Wright seems to be saying that one cannot fight and win in the United States, that one can only become an expatriate.

Richard Wright's white novel, *Savage Holiday,* deals with another aspect of the expatriate pattern which I mentioned earlier: removal or escape or withdrawal from whatever is undesirable or unpleasant as generated by the interplay of personality and society. We know that one reason for a person's becoming an expatriate rests in his need to reject what has already rejected him.

Erskin Fowler is white. He is the social, financial and political opposite to Cross Damon. Fowler is the involved, responsible

American who is a Mason, a Rotarian, a Sunday School Superintendent, who stands six-foot tall, hulking and muscular with "a Lincoln-like, quiet, stolid face."[11] Moreover, he has $40,000 in cash, and he is about to receive a considerable yearly pension as he retires at age 43. Only one matter clouds this attractive reality: he is not retiring, but is being retired, or from an expatriate's point of view, rejected. At his retirement banquet, with which the novel opens, Fowler cannot abide the pretense. He excuses himself to go to the men's room, but in reality, he flees:

> Yes; Erskin had fled. . . . A sudden sense of outrage had made him decide that he would no longer be a party to his own defeat. And what was making him so angry and disgusted with himself was that, at the last moment, instead of hurling a monkey wrench into Warren's smoothly organized machinery of falsehood, he had a failure of nerve, had collaborated in the game of make-believe. . . . He was alone. . . . In fleeing from that banquet room, he had been really trying to flee from himself; that banquet room had been an objective symbolization of a reality which he, at that moment, had wanted more than anything else in the world to avoid.[12]

Erskin Fowler's being the absolute contract to Cross Damon is not the only other-side-of-the-coin quality to this novel. It is ultimately the anti-expatriate novel, except in one aspect: Movement to the city. Fowler was born in Atlanta, but instead of going North on his own, he was brought there by his aunt. In addition, the one woman in the novel with whom Fowler is involved has moved from the provincialism of Pittsburgh and Altoona to New York City. What is of greater interest is Richard Wright's need to create a hero who is trapped by freedom, not only trapped, but terrified by it; just as Cross Damon is ultimately destroyed by his need to be free, Erskin Fowler is destroyed by enforced freedom. It is a form of rejection which he is incapable of handling. As we know, Fowler has been forced to retire:

> Work had . . . given Erskin his livelihood and conferred upon him the approval of his fellow-men. . . . Now, involuntarily reprieved, each week, six full new Sundays suddenly loomed terrifyingly before him and he had to find a way to outwit that rejected part of him that his (occupation) had helped to incarcerate so long and successfully. He was trapped in freedom. How could he again make a foolproof prison of himself for all his remaining days?[13]

Freedom as terror in the fictional Erskin Fowler is precisely the kind of terror which Wright himself felt during his first six months in France and which he was to feel at other times during his expatriation when the quality of the free style of life in France prevented him from working, from writing and creating. The frustration was unbearable, and in fact, it stimulated his return to the States in the opening months of 1947. Wright was to say: " 'The things [he] wanted to get done [were] not done .... Everything over [in France took] a long, long time.' The French people simply had no sense of time as he knew it.' "[14] On another occasion he wrote in his diary: "I love this French mentality sometimes, but not always. Not when practical matters are concerned. . . . I love leisure, but not the kind of leisure that leaves a nation of beggars and cheats." And he was to add, "I'm thirty-nine years old . . . And not much work done. I . . . feel . . . tired from too much worry about petty things."[15]

The theme of rejection, for our purposes, is important. Richard Wright as a black man in America has been rejected. How to get back in is the question. Or even better, how to get in in the first place? "The facts of Negro life (sic), constitute a great body of facts of importance about mankind in general. But white America won't accept it (sic). I think Europeans will accept and understand what I'm saying and then it will filter back to America from Paris and London and Rome."[16] What Wright is saying is obvious: the black man is of vital importance to civilization, but America does not know it. Wright will educate America to the worth of the black man; then, America will stop rejecting the black man and accept him, as he is accepted in Europe. What is of interest for this paper is Wright's turn to Europe to find a climate receptive to and able to understand the plight of the black man, as viewed by Expatriate Richard Wright; it is precisely the same reasoning that prompted the first generation of expatriates to return to Europe to escape the gross, unaesthetic, unreceptive new United States.

The hero of *The Long Dream*, Rex "Fishbelly" Tucker, is, at the close of the novel, in an airplane on his way to Paris and expatriation. He is there because to have remained in his world in Mississippi would have meant death. Having viewed his world as established in the novel, Fishbelly had no real choice. Either he left, or he played Russian roulette with a gun in which every chamber held a bullet.

The novel contains several examples of the American attitude that freedom is associated with movement away from the source of pressure. As an adolescent, Fishbelly was jailed overnight for trespassing; his thoughts upon being released started his thinking about running away:

Oh, if only he could flee to some place where he was not known, where people would accept him as a boy. . . . It was the first time that such a thought had entered his head and it frightened him.[17]

Shortly thereafter, he became ashamed of his father, wondering "Oh, if only he could run off and never look at his father again! But where would he go? How would he live?"[18] When the final confrontation with the Whites came, Fishbelly thought again of movement, this time specifically to the North and expatriation: "The naked fact was that there was nothing left for them but flight . . . Where? North? No. He could be extradited . . . Then maybe to a foreign country where people spoke another language, ate other foods, had alien habits."[19]

The popular belief that France and Paris allow the freedom which Fishbelly longs for is spoken of in a number of ways in the novel. First, as Fishbelly and his teen-age friends discuss service in the armed forces, they utter the cliches, the hearsay, the great hopes for equality popularly associated with France:

"We'll git a chance to go to Paris, mebee," opined Zeke.
"I done hear of that cool town," Fishbelly sighed.
"Man, they say the wine's bitter and women's sweet in Paris," Zeke smiled.
"They say in Paris white folks and black folks walk down the street *together*," Tony sang in a tone of frightened hope.[20]

That hopeful wishing becomes a reality for Fishbelly when he receives a letter from Zeke who is in service in France:

Man, Gay Paree is some burg. . . . Paris is cool. Paris is crazy. These frogs over here even know about rock and roll. And what they don't know about jazz you can put in a thimble. Man, you ought to see these French cats go. The Frenchies can jitterbug from way back. . . . Man, you must be a killer-diller! Why don't you come to Paris and spend some of your money? Living's cheap over here and you sure would like these crazy broads. Man, these blond chicks will go to bed with a guy who's black as the ace of spades and laugh and call it Black Market. Man, it's mad. You know what I mean. . . . I'll be glad when I get out of the army, cause I'm thinking of settling down for a spell in good old Paris."[21]

Zeke's letter is pertinent. As I noted above, the expatriates of the 1920's returned to Europe for a number of reasons, among them, cheaper living and a certain hedonistic attitude toward life which one does not associate, or at least did not associate at the time of the publication of *The Long Dream*, with life in United States. Zeke's reference to cheap living and easy sex is quite what the expatriates of the 20's were looking for. The opportunity to have "blond chicks" and cheap living is as attractive to a white man as it is to a black man, the point being that the materialistic values of expatriate living are part of an American syndrome, white and black, that has been spelled out in literature by American men of letters from Washington Irving to Richard Wright. What is of added interest in Zeke's letter is Wright's including information about French adoption of mediums of expression which are strongly associated with the American Negro: Rock and Roll, Jazz and Jitterbugging.

Richard Wright, Countee Cullen, James Baldwin, Louis Armstrong, Sidney Bechet and countless numbers of unnamed famous and little known black Americans have joined with multitudes of white Americans in the expatriate experience. Wright's later life and later works contain, it seems to me, sufficient evidence of the expatriate pattern to utilize it to darken the curriculum of American literature.

FOOTNOTES

1. Ernest Earnest, *Expatriates and Patriots.* Durham: Duke University Press, 1968, p. 252.
2. Constance Webb, *Richard Wright.* New York: G. P. Putnam's Sons, 1968, p. 242. My source for all biographical data.
3. *Ibid.,* 245, 247.
4. *Ibid.,* 263-291.
5. Richard Wright, *The Outsider.* New York: Perennial Library, 1965, p. 5.
6. *Ibid.,* p. 6.
7. *Ibid.,* p .69.
8. *Ibid.,* p. 88.
9. *Ibid.,* pp. 203, 206.
10. *Ibid.,* p. 277.
11. Richard Wright, *Savage Holiday.* New York: Award Books, 1965, p. 13.
12. *Ibid.,* pp. 20, 21, 22.
13. *Ibid.,* pp. 32, 33.
14. Webb, p. 253.
15. *Ibid.,* p. 277.
16. *Ibid.,* p. 251.
17. Richard Wright, *The Long Dream.* New York: Doubleday, 1958, p. 131.
18. *Ibid.,* p. 147.
19. *Ibid.,* p. 259.
20. *Ibid.,* p. 254.
21. *Ibid.,* pp. 259, 260.

"ANOTHER COUNTRY" AND THE SENSE OF SELF*
by
Elliott M. Schrero

In a well-known essay, Eldridge Cleaver attacks James Baldwin for his inadequately black identity: for refusing to seek in the heart of Africa answers to the questions: *Who am I? From what root do I spring? In what mental and cultural soil can I, must I grow?*[1] Whether or not Cleaver's attack is justified, the point it raises penetrates to the core of our contemporary cultural and political agony. It is thus of some interest to examine how questions of identity figure in Baldwin's *Another Country,* a novel in which they are deeply implicated. The interest of this enterprise grows, I think, if Baldwin's novel is compared to another significant work equally infused with the theme of identity but approaching it from a point of view very different from his. The novel I propose to use as this touchstone is William Faulkner's *Absalom, Absalom!*

My warrant for doing so is not that the two novels have any direct historical or intellectual relationship. Nor is it simply that both novels raise the question of racial identity by dealing with sexual pairings across the color line. Nor again, is it the symmetry of comparing a Southern white consciousness with Baldwin's troubled Harlem-bred sense of life. All these grounds exist; but the best justification for viewing the two novels in relation to each other is the reciprocal light they shed on the possibilities for experiencing the fact of one's identity, or the problem of it.

For their handling of racial identity, it is easy enough to indict both novels if we are content to look at isolated passages or situa-

---

*Revised version of paper delivered at NEMLA meeting, Philadelphia, 1971, as part of Rider College panel.

tions. Thus one can argue that *In Another Country* Ida Scott's love for Vivaldo Moore expresses Baldwin's inability to respect black manhood. In some eyes, the proper attitude for Baldwin to adopt toward Ida would have been the contempt expressed by the bass player at Small's Paradise, rather than the neutral or even approving regard Baldwin seems to accord her. Yet if we argue that Ida acts out Baldwin's self-abnegation toward whites, how shall we weigh her hostility toward them? If we are to form our judgments on the basis of isolated aspects of a novel, or on what seem to be indicative passages, we shall have to deal with Ida's remark that white people are "too cowardly even to know what they [have] done" to black people, an indictment echoed by Cass Silenski's description of the United States as "not a country at all," but merely "a collection of football players and Eagle Scouts. Cowards" (pp. 350, 342). Similarly, one can accuse Faulkner of racism if one attends simply to the close of *Absalom, Absalom!*, where Shrevlin McCannon sees the meaning of the Sutpen tragedy in the survival of Jim Bond, the idiot of mixed racial origins, whose kind, says Shrevlin, will some day conquer the western hemisphere, so that, he says, "in a few thousand years, I who regard you will also have sprung from the loins of African kings" (p. 378). But the mention of African kings does not sound like white Southern racism.

I raise these questions not because I believe them to be critical problems, but rather to suggest the usefulness of taking the whole of each novel into account in any effort to compare and interpret their underlying ideologies. The two novels, it happens, are constructed on quite different plans. The structure of *Absalom, Absalom!* is adumbrated in Mr. Compson's observation that the figures of the Sutpen story appear "in this shadowy attentuation of time possessing new heroic proportions . . . inscrutable and serene, against the turgid background of a horrible and bloody mischancing of human affairs" (p. 101). Such a description reminds one of Sophocles or Euripides; and the analogy is the stronger because Mr. Compson, as well as Quentin, Schrevlin, and Rosa Coldfield, offer diverse choric commentaries as they tell or piece together the story. Emerging fully only toward the close of the novel, in a reconstruction by Shrevlin and Quentin, the basic action is indeed a tragedy along classic lines, with peripety and discovery and tragic deeds.

In outline, the action of *Absalom, Absalom!* is straightforward and distinct, but it makes a quite different impression in the novel because of the way it is presented. It is told and retold, from different viewpoints, and with various degrees of completeness: in retrospect, as remembered by those on its periphery, as told by witnesses long after the events, as revealed in an old letter, and as reconstructed by latter-day minds attempting to make sense of it. A very different type of narrative structure confronts us in *Another Country*. Here all is clear-cut; but instead of one line of action, we have four, involving pairs of lovers variously doomed or damned: Rufus Scott and Leona, Ida Scott and Vivaldo Moore, Richard and Cass Silenski, Eric and Yves. Rufus Scott and Leona, black man and white woman, destroy each other despite their mutual love; and their fate throws a shadow across the other pairings. Rufus' sister Ida and Vivaldo Moore, a white man, live together; but their relationship suffers from Ida's bitterness against whites and from Vivaldo's white man's inability to understand the experience which produces that bitterness. Ida, in pursuit of a career, sleeps with another white man because he has the power to promote her fortune as a singer. Meanwhile, Cass Silenski, disillusioned with her husband Richard, seeks out the homosexual Eric, has a brief affair with him, and then confesses to Richard. Ida likewise confesses her infidelity to Vivaldo. As for Eric, he gives up his affair with Cass, for it confirms him in his homosexuality, and awaits reunion with his lover, Yves, who will shortly arrive from France. By the end of the novel, Cass and Richard, Ida and Vivaldo, Eric and Yves are more or less reunited after their physical or spiritual separations, but not happily or permanently. Richard threatens to divorce Cass; Ida predicts that she will never marry Vivaldo; Eric feels that someday Yves must abandon him. Cass, Vivaldo, and Eric have all confronted truths about their lives that they did not want to know, and each has grown wiser but also closer to despair. The unity of the action lies in the analogous problems faced by each couple and in the actual or impending failure of each relationship.

The quality of this unity — the impression it makes on our sensibilities — depends to a great extent on the sentiments and comments of Cass, Ida, Vivaldo, and Eric, just as the choral commentary of the various narrators of *Absalom, Absalom!* determines the distinctive quality of that novel. In these sentiments and comments, of course, ideology comes to the fore. The commentary selects an angle of vision from which to view action and character, perceive proportions and relations, interpret causes and consequences, and estimate the values at stake. But there are two striking differences in the situations which the persons in each novel interpret for us. Although both novels present forbidden relationships, violating racial as well as sexual taboos, in *Absalom, Absalom!* some of the relationships bear fruit — bitter or bruised fruit, but, all the same, links to posterity Sutpen fathers Charles Bon, who fathers Charles Etienne St. Velery Bon, who fathers Jim Bond. The relationships in *Another Country,* on the contrary, remain barren save for the marriage of Cass and Richard Silenski. There is no sense of remote progenitors; one hears something of parents and elders, but not very much. Ida speaks of her parents' grief at her brother's death, but her sense of her own destiny is not determined by any sense of heritage. For Vivaldo, the mention of family and home invariably suggests alienation.

In *Absalom, Absalom!,* however, all personal relationships, belong to a march of generations, take their places in a process, with a past and a future, a heritage bequeathed and to bequeath. This points up the basic difference between the situations presented by the two novels. Personal relationships in *Absalom, Absalom!* belong to a social process which is deeply historical. The present is evolved from the past, but the past remains embedded within it; the present, moreover, generates a future, which, though hidden, is implicit in the present, exerting at times the pull of an obscure destiny. Personal relationships in *Another Country* are also part of a social process, as we shall see; but the process is contemporary, cut off from the past that produced it and lacking any intelligible future. In short, Faulkner's fictive persons are imprisoned in the South, an historical entity rather than a geographical one; Baldwin's are trapped in the twentieth century.

From this difference flows a second. To see oneself as part of an historical process, as entrusted by the past with a legacy for the future, is to have identity. The South in *Absalom, Absalom!* confers it on black and white, because the South is one's matrix for being. A merely contemporary present, the present of *Another Country,* cannot confer identity. A merely contemporary present actually confuses identity, because contrary impulses coexist without any authority — either of past heroes and models, or of a future entrusted to one's hands — with which to resist the internalized contradictions of society. Both kinds of world, the world of the South and the world of the merely contemporary, can drive a man to suicide, given the right mix of circumstance and character. Quentin Compson ultimately dies rejecting time and history just as Rufus Scott dies rejecting his senseless present, although for Quentin's death we must turn, of course, to *The Sound and the Fury.*

"ANOTHER COUNTRY" AND THE SENSE OF SELF

Without past to illuminate the present, one must seek illumination elsewhere. People in *Another Country,* as the title partly suggests, reach across culture, across race, across boundaries of the permissible in love, to find a saving truth or at least a refuge from the world into which they are born. For the most part, however, the truth is disheartening. After living in Paris, Eric sees New York in a gloomy light:

> It was not possible in this city, as it had been for Eric in Paris, to take a long and peaceful walk at any hour of the day or night, dropping in for a drink at a bistro or flopping oneself down at a sidewalk cafe — the half-dozen grim parodies of sidewalk cafes to be found in New York were not made for flopping. It was a city without oases, run entirely, insofar, at least, as human perception could tell, for money; and its citizens seemed to have lost entirely any sense of their right to renew themselves. Whoever, in New York, attempted to cling to this right, lived in New York in exile — in exile from the life around him; and this paradoxically, had the effect of placing him in perpetual danger of being forever banished from any real sense of himself (p. 267).

In an earlier passage, the horrors of life in New York strike Eric with special force during the first days of his return from Paris:

> New York seemed very strange indeed. It might, almost, for strange barbarity of manner and custom, for the sense of danger and horror barely sleeping beneath the rough, gregarious surface, have been some impenetrably exotic city of the East. So superbly was it in the present, that it seemed to have nothing to do with the passage of time . . . (p. 195).

Eric feels that the dominant fact about New York is its despair. "This note of despair, of buried despair, was insistently, constantly struck. It stalked all the New York avenues, roamed all the New York streets. . . . He could not escape the feeling that a kind of plague was raging, though it was officially and publicly and privately denied. Even the young seemed blighted" (p. 196). The general blight manifests itself as a continual fight against isolation. "One was continually being jostled," Eric notes, "yet longed, at the same time, for the sense of others . . .; and if one was never — it was the general complaint — left alone in New York, one had, still, to fight very hard not to perish of loneliness. This fight, carried on in so many different ways, created the strange climate of the city" (p. 195).

Compare Eric, jostled by flesh-and-blood contemporaries, yet almost perishing of loneliness, with Quentin Compson, who early in *Absalom, Absalom!* is described as being two persons — "the

Quentin Compson preparing for Harvard in the South, the deep South dead since 1865, peopled with garrulous, outraged, baffled ghosts, listening, having to listen, to one of the ghosts which had refused to lie still even longer than most had, telling him about old ghost-times; and the Quentin Compson who was still too young to deserve yet to be a ghost, but nevertheless having to be one for all that, since he was born and bred in the deep South the same as she was" (p. 9). Quentin is inescapably bound to the ghosts of the Old South; we read that "his very body was an empty hall echoing with sonorous defeated names; he was not a being, an entity, he was a commonwealth. He was a barracks filled with stubborn back-looking ghosts" (p. 12).

These back-looking ghosts are specific to the South; they define its sickness, because, as Quentin realizes, they are "still recovering, even forty-three years afterward, from the fever which had cured the disease, waking from the fever without even knowing that it had been the fever itself which they had fought against and not the sickness, looking with stubborn recalcitrance backward beyond the fever and into the disease with actual regret, weak from the fever yet free of the disease and not even aware that the freedom was that of impotence" (p. 12). If we ask what is the disease mentioned here, a passage in Faulkner's story "The Bear" furnishes the answer. In that story Isaac McCaslin tells the history of the South, from the first alienation of its land by chieftans such as Ikkemotubbe. Trying to account for God's purpose in letting the land fall into the hands of exploiting white men, Isaac McCaslin says, "Maybe it was more than justice that only the white man's blood was available and capable to raise the white man's curse, more than vengeance when . . . [God] used the blood which had brought in the evil to destroy the evil as doctors use fever to burn up fever, poison to slay poison" (p. 259). The evil, as other parts of this passage make clear, is slavery. The fever, here and in *Absalom, Absalom!* is the Civil War.

The evil, I have said, is slavery; but it would be more accurate to say that *Absalom, Absalom!* presents the evil as a social system and a culture whose most acute manifestation is slavery. On the social plane, the evil appears as a rigid caste system, which contributes to its own destruction by putting power into unworthy hands — "generals who should not have been generals, who were generals not through training in contemporary methods or aptitude for learning them, but by the divine right to say 'Go there' conferred upon them by an absolute caste system" (p 345). On the private and individual plane, the evil is epitomized in Thomas Sutpen, whom Rosa Coldfield describes, in her vindictiveness, as a man "with valor and strength but without pity or honor." With such men to buttress the cause of the South, "it is any wonder," she asks, "that Heaven saw fit to let us lose?" (p. 20).

This sickness of the South, as dramatized in Thomas Sutpen and his family, differs from the sickness that at one point in *Another Country* Baldwin calls the "twentieth-century" torment" (p. 278). Vivaldo defines the twentieth-century malady as a loss of a sense of form. "When people no longer knew that a mystery could only be approached through form, people became — what the people of this time and place had become, what he had become. They perished . . . in isolation, passively, or actively together, in mobs, thirsting and seeking for, and eventually reeking of blood" (p. 255). Cass Silenski puts it a little differently. She says of her husband, "He doesn't have any real work to do, that's his trouble, that's the trouble with this whole unspeakable time and place" (pp. 341-42). And then she goes on to draw the consequence that people in this time and place are empty-hearted.

Now, from one point of view, what is described in *Another Country* is a condition directly the reverse of the spiritual and social sickness depicted in *Absalom, Absalom!* In a caste system, the one thing people do not lack is real work to do; and, far from lacking order and form, they suffer from an excess of formality; formality that replaces individuals with stereotypes. Replacing individuals with stereotypes is one mode of acting without real honor and often without even a semblance of pity and compassion. The caste system of the South, culminating in violent injustices to black people, reflects a failure of the heart in the individuals who live by that system. For it reverses the intention of God, defined by Isaac McCaslin in "The Bear," in leading white men into the New World. God, says Isaac McCaslin, "discovered to them a new world where a nation of people could be founded in humility and pity and sufferance and pride of one to another," where men could "hold the earth mutual and intact in the communal anonymity of brotherhood" (pp. 258-59). Instead of which, white men like Isaac McCaslin's grandfather, Carothers McCaslin, substituted for brotherhood the slavery of other men, and for communal anonymity the absolute caste distinctions that drove Thomas Sutpen into a career of furious and unremitting violation of the lives of others.

It is clear, then, that the different social sicknesses analyzed in *Absalom, Absalom!* and *Another Country* manifest themselves in the failings of the individuals whose lives are depicted in these novels. The failure of true honor and pride and pity and compassion in Faulkner's novel has its counterpart in the empty-heartedness described by Cass Silenski, one form of which is alienation. This is the general sickness in *Another Country;* it afflicts everybody. The paradox is that all the people in Baldwin's novel seek to cure their alienation, or at least assuage it, by a plunge into what is alien. The married woman forsakes her husband's bed for a homosexual man; the homosexual American flees to the homosexual Frenchman; the Frenchman flees to America, that exotic country; the black man cleaves to the white woman; the white man, to the black woman. This cleaving to the alien is their experience of love. The pursuit of the alien defines both the sought-after remedy and the reason for its failure. If the malady of twentieth-century man, suffered in its most extreme form in New York City, is emptiness of heart, then the cure might well be emotional union. But at the heart of love, experienced as the pursuit of the alien, is the paradox that to love what is alien is to struggle vainly to achieve union with what is irremediably remote. Eric, walking with Cass Silenski through the "icy and angular jungle" of the Museum of Modern Art in New York, wishes "that he could rescue her, that it was in his power to rescue her and make her life less hard." But he realizes that he can do nothing for her. "It was only love that could accomplish the miracle of making a life bearable — only love, and love itself mostly failed" (p. 340).

This, then, is the universal sickness in *Another Country.* But there is also a special sickness, the sickness inflicted on black people by their treatment at the hands of whites. The black person is doubly alienated; and his plight is described to both Cass and Vivaldo by Ida, although she knows that neither of them can fully understand what she tells them. The bleakness of the prognosis for all these people is unrelieved by hope. The very terms of the cure specified for their suffering suggest that the cure must fail.

No such despairing conclusion need be drawn from *Absalom, Absalom!* If the failure of a social system is a failure of the heart's virtues, the cure for its crimes and follies must be the discovery and resuscitation of those virtues. One means of this resuscitation is to understand truly how the past survives in the present, to establish a bond of love and reverence for predecessors from whom one received the torch. This truth is partly perceived by Thomas Sutpen; only partly, however, and therein lies the nature of the tragedy, according to Quentin Compson. "Sutpen's trouble," he says, "was innocence. All of a sudden he discovered, not what he wanted to do but what he just had to do whether he wanted to or not, because if he did not do it he knew that he could never live with himself for the rest of his life, never live with what all the men and women that had died to make him had left inside of him for him to pass on, with all the dead ones waiting and watching to see if he was going to do it right, fix things right so that he would be able to look in the face not only the old dead ones but all the living ones that would come after him when he would be one of the dead" (p. 220). This is honor; the trouble, in Sutpen's case, is that the right is misconceived, and is divorced from pity and compassion. A tradition rightly understood can bring salvation, as for old Isaac McCaslin; misunderstood and misinterpreted, it destroys individuals and social systems. Faulkner finds the keys to interpretation in the old heroic virtues — "love and honor and pity and pride and compassion and sacrifice," without which, Faulkner said in his famous Nobel Prize speech, "any story is ephemeral and doomed."

To seek the models of these virtues in the Southern past seems perfectly natural, if one is born in the South, and one is white. A similar logic would seem to dictate that Baldwin should seek strength and virtue in his own heritage, which for Eldridge Cleaver must be defined as African. And Cleaver would probably argue that the desolation of Baldwin's fictive persons in *Another Country* confirms his diagnosis of Baldwin's own psychic ills. But perhaps there is more to be said. The sickness of the inhabitants of *Another Country* afflicts white people as well as black; it is more than a symptom of racial oppression. Its origins are in the general culture, and its action is on man, not on races as such. Baldwin is not the first to recognize this condition; Emile Durkheim named it long ago as *anomie*. The cure for this condition is not, in Baldwin's view, so easily found in one's heritage if one is black and was born in North America; for a man's heritage is not only what he wishes to affirm as the seal of his identity, but also what he involuntarily carries forward from his past, an unpaid balance, it may be, of sorrow. It is this burden that Leo Poundhammer, in *Tell Me How Long the Train's Been Gone,* measures in the self-hatred of those young black men whom he analyzes as the victims of a history which their enemies had written for them:

> They had been formed by the images made of them by those who had had the deepest necessity to despise them. The bitterly contemptuous uses to which they had been put by others was the beginning of their history, the key to their lives, and the very

cornerstone of their identities: exactly like those who had first maligned them, they saw what their history had taught them to see. I did not know then, and I do not know now if one ever sees more than that. If one ever does, it can only be because one has learned to read one's history and resolved to step out of the book (p. 146).

FOOTNOTES

1. See Eldridge Cleaver, "Notes on a Native Son," in *Soul on Ice* (New York: McGraw-Hill, 1968; rpt. New York: Dell, n. d.), pp. 97-111. Page references to the writings of James Baldwin or William Faulkner are to the following editions: James Baldwin, *Another Country* (New York: Dial, 1962; rpt. New York: Dell, 1970); *Tell Me How Long the Train's Been Gone* (New York: Dial, 1968; rpt New York: Dell, 1969); William Faulkner, *Absalom, Absalom!,* Modern Library, 271 (New York: Random House, 1951); "The Bear," in *Go Down Moses,* Modern Library, 175 (New York: Random House, 1955), pp. 101-331.

"DUTCHMAN" AND "THE SLAVE" COMPANIONS IN REVOLUTION

by

JOHN LINDBERG

LeRoi Jones' two plays, *Dutchman* and *The Slave,* published together as one book, offer many striking parallels, each the reverse of the other, in character and theme. These reverse parallels are so strong that the plays, though published as distinct works, make sense as a single piece. The two important themes are the theme of search and the theme of sanity. They develop through the time-lapse between plays, because each play gives a stage in Jones' view of black revolution as one phase of a continuing race-war.

I

Many obvious reversed parallels bring us to an enriched understanding of the themes of search and sanity. Both plays present a race-war, and in *Dutchman* the white wins, and in *The Slave* the black wins. The winners are opposite sexes representing opposed cultural goals. The black loser in the first play is a would-be revolutionist who prefers the comfortable role of an artist-intellectual following white models. The black winner in the second play is a one-time artist-intellectual who has rejected white models to achieve violent black-nationalist goals.

The white victor-woman in *Dutchman* imposes her values on her black male victim. The black victor-male in *The Slave* forces his triumphant philosophy on his white ex-wife. Lula, Western culture's bitch-goddess, first entices and then denies the sexual urge of Clay, whose death is only the final version of his emasculated life. Walker Vessels taunts his ex-wife's white husband with impotence, and the artillery barrage of Walker's vigorous black soldiers kills the white woman he loved and then rejected when she could not continue to love him as he worked for a black victory. Walker with his penis-gun replaces Lulu with her gelding knife. His last name, Vessels, has male erotic meaning to contrast with the pun in the name of his white male victim, Easley. And his first name, Walker, has the purposefulness missing in the malleable character suggested by the name Clay of his black opposite in the first play.

How do these reversed parallels help us understand the themes of search and sanity? Only when we view the plays as complementary do we know the full meaning of several actions and lines. Lulu enters eating an apple, in the role of temptress, searching for knowledge and corrupting her men by insisting they help her search in her own way. She invites Clay with words echoing the Fall from Innocence, when Adam and Eve discover their nakedness: "I . . . saw you staring . . . down in the vicinity of my ass and legs"; "Eating apples together is always the first step"; "What've you got that jacket and tie on in all this heat for?" Clay is only the next in a series of relationships she has discarded as phony: "Walked down the aisle . . . searching you out"; "Dull, dull, dull. I bet you thing I'm exciting"; "I told you I didn't know all about *you* . . . you're a well-known type"; "My hair is turning gray. A gray hair for each year and type I've come through"; "Everything you say is wrong. That's what makes you so attractive."

> [Searching aimlessly through her bag. She begins to talk breathlessly, with a light and silly tone] All stories are whole stories. All of 'em. Our whole story . . . nothing but change. How could things go on like that forever? Huh?
> [Slaps him on the shoulder, begins finding things in her bag, taking them out and throwing them over her shoulder into the aisle.] Except I do go on as I do. Apples and long walks with deathless intelligent lovers.

Searching through her bag and discarding things — we imagine symbols of dominance like wallet, car keys, lipstick, compact, comb, sexy-cover paperbacks filling the air — she has exhausted her repertoire of cultural plays, and confronts Clay on what she considers to be ultimate ground, the question of his sincerity. This confrontation is the climax of the play. When Clay turns to stone defiance, her only recourse to protect herself from her own ignorance is to kill him. She has always looked for a master, but Clay has loved her white world so well he is unwary and falls to her surprise knife.

The best lines are Lulu's. She is the protagonist, the hysterical bitch of white values. But Clay's own search has fed her the lines, because he has admired success that she can scorn. He wallows in lubricious pleasure at the picture of himself at a party with a white beauty, on a long delicately delaying evening ending in bed with her. She makes him sneer at his name, his parents, their dreams, and their past: "Take your pick. Jackson, Johnson, or Williams"; "My grandfather was a night watchman"; "My mother was a Republican"; "Plantations were big open whitewashed places like heaven, and everybody on 'em was grooved to be there. Just strummin' and hummin' all day"; "And that's how the blues was born." Everything he says justifies her contempt:

> LULU. . . . About your manhood, what do you think? What do you think we've been talking about all this time?
> CLAY. Well, I didn't know it was that. That's for sure. Every other thing in the world but that.

Thus Lulu can rage at his hypocrisy and taunt him by claiming to know more about blacks than he does, with her insulting invitation to the dance: "You middle-class black bastard. Forget your social-working mother for a few seconds and let's knock stomachs."

The climax of the play, the confrontation which now occurs, relates the search theme to the sanity theme. Both Clay and Lulu have searched for themselves by playing roles, and now they test their final roles. Lulu has become a destroyer in her search for integrity. She is past sanity though sanity is her search: "Red trains cough Jewish underwear for keeps! Expanding smells of silence. Gravy snot whistling like sea birds. Clay. Clay, you got to break out. Don't sit there dying the way they want you to die." In these lines Lulu actually begs Clay to save her from her own kind. But when he is only embarrassed, she makes the mistake of taunting him with his acceptance of white values and makes him speak the truth they have both avoided: "If I'm a middle-class fake white man . . . let me be. And let me be in the way I want . . .You fuck some black man, and right away you're an expert on black people. What a lotta shit that is." For the moment Clay refuses to accept the lies Lulu uses to "control the world . . . I lie all the time. Draw your own conclusions."

But she wants to believe in her verson of funky black vitality so she can deny Clay's view of the blacks' arts as an escapist sub-limation of hate for dominant whites, a response as ineffective as his own imitation of whites:

> Some kind of bastard literature . . . all it needs is a simple knife thrust. . . . A whole people of neurotics, struggling to keep from being sane. And the only thing that would cure the neurosis would be your murder. . . . But who needs it? I'd rather be a

fool. Insane. Safe with my words, and no deaths, and clean, hard thoughts urging me to new conquests.

In choosing insanity he accepts Lulu's false view of blacks, knowing it is false, confirms her in error, and accepts the knife thrust he knows could be his to give when Lulu kills him rather than admit she has wasted her life fighting unreal enemies. For she has not won. Clay knows with a foresight of his reincarnation in Walker that the blacks are truly sane: "My people. They don't need me to claim them. They got legs and arms of their own. . . . They don't need all those words. They don't need any defense. . . . They'll murder you, and have very rational explanations."

II

Clay's choice of insanity places the motivation of the characters in both plays outside of individual values, "[p]ersonal insanities." Lulu seems to accept this relative view of personal responsibility when she says playfully: "We'll pretend that we are both anonymous beauties smashing along through the city's entrails." The opening stage directions read: *"In the flying underbelly of the city. . . . Underground. The subway heaped in modern myth";* men are caught in the development of their institutions.

History seen as a black revolutionary process is the value-reference in both plays, a reference that shows clearly to help us grasp the significance of the action in either play only when we consider both plays together. Clay has foreseen the eventual victory of his own people, whom Walker, in the next play, leads to the brink of that victory. Walker has rejected Grace, his white ex-wife, because she cannot reconcile his personal love for her with his political action to kill white people. Brad Easley, Grace's new white husband, cannot tolerate Walker's black revolution because it makes impossible "life as a purely anarchic relationship between man and God . . . or man and his work." Walker has grown beyond his role as Brad's pupil. Personal relationships, individual reputation must emerge with the socializing imperative of the black revolution.

The themes of search and sanity appear again in *The Slave* after their first appearance in *Dutchman,* this time in an obvious physical way because the race war is now open. Lulu can no longer knife Clay by surprise. The roles are now actual, not symbolic. Prologuizing, Walker begins: "Whatever the core of our lives. Whatever the deceit. We live where we are, and seek nothing but ourselves. We are liars, and we are murderers." The universal pronoun in these lines states the implicit theme in *Dutchman* that history no longer allows private compromise but throws individuals into public roles. Ideas — personal justifications — no longer have meaning even when honest: "The very rightness stinks a lotta times." "I am an old man," Walker complains, and in the prologue he is older than in the play, because the prologue shows us Walker after he has lived through the play. In the play, he is a liar and murderer to the whites who deny his public role.

For the playing-time of the play Walker has deserted his public role to return to his private past, partly in genuine regret, mainly to break his last ties with his earlier self when he was still a nonhistoric personality. He checks his watch to keep track of the pace of history so he will not be caught by his men on the scene of his shame, his outdated white loyalties. The action of the play speeds up as the bombardment approaches, and Walker finally frees himself from his white past as the house collapses under black shells. He has now shed false roles and lived into his destiny — search and sanity coincide as he makes his way back to his men. But for the space of the play he has returned to an insane part of his life, and the action consists of his trying to explain to Grace and Brad why he is not the liar and murderer they call him.

While working up a climactic scene, Walker plays mock-roles as a stupid darkie, a stage Irishman, a Japanese torturer, because Brad and Grace refuse to take him seriously as a militant leader:

>GRACE. . . . It must be a sick task keeping so many lying separate ugliness together . . . and pretending they're something you've made and understand.
>WALKER. What I can use . . .
>EASLEY. . . . What is this, the pragmatics of war? . . . I thought you meant yourself to be a fantastic idealist? . . .
>WALKER. . . . Now you can call me the hypocritical idealist nigger murderer.

The argument over the girls arises because the whites refuse to believe a killer can love his children. They do not understand when he claims the girls for the black revolutionary future. He agrees with the whites that this future is created by violence and betrayal, and insists that the end justifies the means. Nearly every speech by Grace and Brad in this part of the play uses words like *lying* and *insane*. Walker's sanity is their insanity: "You thought I betrayed you . . . And don't, now . . . start thinking he's disillusioned . . . cynical, or any of these . . . liberal definitions of the impossibility or romanticism of idealism."

At this point the dialogue again places values in the historical destiny of black triumph and rejects conventional morals: "What does it matter if there's more love or beauty [in black victory]? Who the fuck cares? . . . The point is that you had your chance, darling, now these other folks have theirs." And when Brad stresses the ugliness of this idea, Walker again admits that in the past he valued personal ideas but had to give them up as luxuries in the need for revolt: "No social protest . . . right is in the act! And the act itself has some place in the world . . . it makes some place for itself." These words reverse Walker's mockery of non-historical private values when he says in the prologue: "But figure, still, ideas are still in the world. They need judging." And ideas are judged by the act.

No understanding is possible any more between Walker and his whites. His new true role inevitably leads to Brad's death, when Grace repeats four times in a crescendo of horror: "You're an insane man." Grace calls him insane because she is unable to see him as a superman now that he has fulfilled his destiny. His old values must die to make room for his new life: "There is no reason he [Brad] should go out with any kind of dignity. I couldn't allow that." To which Grace repeats three times: "You're out of your mind." And Walker retorts: ". . . being out of your mind is the only thing that qualifies you to stay alive. . . . Easley was in his right mind. . . . That's the reason he's dead." These lines echo the cross-accusations between Lula and Clay with the difference that Walker has consciously passed into the historic personality that Clay foretold for his people.

When we learn that Walker has killed his children, this knowledge completes his reversal of Clay. He has jived Grace and Brad with his assumed role of concerned black parent who risks death to rescue the girls from a life as whites. Lulu had taunted Clay for playing a white role. Walker makes his point by playing a role when it suits his purpose in the argument, but the whites are the deluded ones. And while Clay falls easily to Lulu's knife because he admires her whiteness, Walker kills his children to free himself from all white taint. He has become the man without a past, the stone revolutionist, clay no more.

This totally new man, committed to a historical imperative, has passed beyond conventional human roles. The play opens and closes with stage directions calling for children crying. Walker quotes a Yeats poem ironically, a poem about wounded innocence. But his irony arises from the fact that he no longer copies Yeats by writing poems; he has become the intolerable music Yeats foretells — he has just murdered his children. In the prologue he is unsure of his age, after the success of his revolt. In the play, he admits to Brad that the black revolution may build no better world than the whites have done. He fulfills Brad's dying mockery, for the character of Walker complements that of Clay, and the two plays compose a ritual drama symbolizing LeRoi Jones' conviction that history develops through cycles of race-war.

CARIBBEAN LITERATURE IN ENGLISH: 1949-1970
by
R. M. Lacovia

This review of Caribbean literature in English 1949-1970 focuses mainly on the novel in its cultural setting. After World War II, there occurred a sudden surge in Caribbean literature. (Walcott 1948, Reid 1949, Selvon 1952, Lamming 1953, Mais 1953.) Since then three pace setters have emerged (V. S. Naipaul, Wilson Harris, Edward Brathwaite). This essay mainly examines these three authors.

Neo African Trends:

With his novel *New Day* Victor Reid in 1949 opened new possibilities for the usage of dialect and history. The narrator an old man spans in his memory 1865-1944, he spans the loss of potential self rule in 1865 to the 'new day' 1944 when self rule is regained. Reid's book is a triumph of the arts of the imagination, and Wilson Harris is quite correct when he states "it is my personal view that there does not exist a philosophy of history in the Caribbean correlative to the arts of the imagination."[1]

Temporal v's Spatial Perspective:

For the European time is the measure of movement along a line (linear or circular). This measure is determined by numbers resulting in a spatialization of time — sundials, clocks, etc. The Caribbean[2] is uncertain about his spatial identity, but like ancient Hebrews he is constantly weighed down by time. John Mbiti states that the "religious and social life of the ancient Jew is similar to that of many African societies . . . Some of the obvious differences lie in the fact that Judaism developed a prophetic movement and a messianic expectation, neither of which has any parallels in African traditional background."[3] While the lack of prophetic movement and messianic expectation may be true for traditional African society it is not true for neo African thought in the Caribbean. One has only to point to Bedward, the Garvey movement, the Ras Tafari in Jamaica and the shango cults of Trinidad. As with the ancient Hebrew and traditional African society, the Caribbean focuses on the peculiarity of events, hence time is determined by its contents.

"Time is simply a composition of events which have occurred, those which are taking place now and those which are immediately to occur . . . Time has to be experienced in order to make sense or to become real . . . Time is a composition of events . . . Instead of numerical calendars there are what one would call phenomenal calendars . . . For the people concerned, time is meaningful at the point of the event and not at the mathematical moment."[4]

Chronos v's Kairos:

Chronos is closely related to the European concept of time. It is the uniform time of the cosmic system, and expresses time as measure as applied to movement. The relevant questions are how fast, how frequent, etc. Kairos on the other hand is a critical time, a turning point in history (Exodus of the Ancient Hebrew, Middle passage of the Caribbean) and occurs in a special temporal position which negates chance. *New Day* is written with Kairos in mind. "Is what it you want? Change, you want to change God's order? You and those others can no' wait for Jehovah's plan?"[5] Chance happens in an obscure way, an occurrence of events that could have happened at any time. Kairos is the favourable time which must be apprehended as such through historical insight. "Chris Langley was the one who led the talk that now was the time. Garth did no' disagree with him, but held say it should be done with wisdom."[6] The specific question is when? At what time? There is a time to be cautious. "He does no' talk with his mouth too far before him . . . No so Chris and the rest of them. So now they are caged behind the wire . . . Many months passed while Garth walked on tiptoe and covered his mouth, for power was no' yet with him."[7] Continued in this concept are three distinct but related elements, (a) the right time as opposed to any time, (b) the time of crisis, a time when decisions have to be made, (c) the time when an opportunity for accomplishing some purpose has arisen. "To everything there is a season, and a time to every purpose under the heaven . . . A time to get, and a time to lose . . . a time to keep silence, and a time to speak . . . a time of war and a time of peace."[8] Roger Mais in his first novel *The Hills Were Joyful Together* contrasts chronos and kairos in series of juxtaposed passages: His novel *Brother Man* is totally concerned with Kairos. The chief character being Brother Man a member of the Ras Tafari sect, a messianic movement which postulates Ethiopia as the promised land. Mais not only portrays Brother Man as a Christ figure, he also follows rather closely the story of the events leading up to the crucifixion and resurrection.

Zamani and Sasa Time Concept:

In neo African thought Chronos becomes the Zamani period and Kairos the Sasa period. For the western world time has an indefinite past, an immediate present and an infinite future. Above all time moves forward. For the African according to Mbiti, time moves backward. The Sasa period is when and where people exist. It includes (a) future events which fall within the rhythm of nature and are predictably certain shortly to occur. (b) events in the process of realization, and (c) memories of personal or community experiences. The Sasa period is when and where people exist. It includes (a) future events which fall within the rhythm of nature and are predictably certain shortly to occur. (b) events in the process of realization, and (c) memories of personal or community experiences. The Sasa period feeds into and disappears into the Zamani period which overlaps it. In the West a man is dead when he is physically dead. Not so for the African. After physical death the individual remains alive as long as he is remembered by one who was acquainted with him. He remains in the Sasa period, in other words he retains his individuality until the last person who knew him by acquaintance dies.

In answer to the question "Who am I?" the African replies, "I am my memories, and I am, because there are memories." Wilson Harris, by far the greatest innovator of the Caribbean writers, has made extensive explorations of memory and the Sasa and Zamani periods. With considerable technical virtuosity he explored the Sasa period in his Guyana quartet (his first four novels) "We had hardly turned into the bank when a fleet of canoes devoured us. Faces pressed upon us from land and water. The news was confirmed like wild-fire. We were the news. It was ourselves who were the news. Everyone remembered that not so long ago this self-same crew had been drowned to a man in the rapids below the Mission."[9] He condemns the western obscession with chronos. "Much of the character of civilization . . . has been geared to this static clock which obviously seeks to shape its material, all its human material, into time tables of defensive capital, defensive labour and other territorial imperatives. That is why the catalogues of deeds compiled by historians conform to dead time that measures man as a deriviative industry-making animal, tool-making animal, weapon-making animal."[10] What is needed is a different orientation to time. "The quest for an inner clock is so necessary in our situation of social and industrial character geared relentlessly to static time . . . that it constitutes a universal, complex and liberating theme."[11] This new concept of time is embodied in his novels. The following lines are from the first two pages of the first novel:

"A horseman appeared on the road coming at a breakneck stride. A shot rang out suddenly, near and yet far as if the wind had been stretched and torn and had started coiling and running in an instant . . . The sun blinded and ruled my living sight but the dead man's eye remained open and obstinate and clear. I dreamt I awoke with one dead seeing eye and one living closed eye . . . Someone rapped on the door of my cell and room. I started on seeing the dream — horseman, tall and spare and hard looking as ever . . . And we looked through the same window of the room together and, through his dead seeing material eye, rather than through my living closed spiritual eye."[12] In his most recently published work, *The Sleepers of Roraima,* Harris has turned to an exploration of the Zamani period, through the re-enactment of Carib myths. Concerning this re-enactment Harris has this to say, "I recalled my boyhood (before World War II broke out) when I often swam at the Fort on the Georgetown foreshore. I reflected also on the observation I made when I was last in Georgetown in 1966: the sea no longer stands where it used to be and the land has grown in its place by six or seven feet. Therefore, if I were to endow the de facto mound or grave which now exists in the foreshore with a figurative meaning beyond the present stasis of reality I might see the ghost of the past (the ghost of my childhood) swimming in dry land. That kind of imagination — which is clearly suspect to the politician — is true of areas of the primitive world and in my conception it corresponds to the architecture of consciousness within which the opaque mound or wall of earth is a relative, not absolute, feature; and the swimmer in dry land witnesses to a fluid room or dimension that was also relative when it occurred."[13]

Historicity

V. S. Naipaul in his book *The Middle Passage* has pungent opinion about the Caribbean area. "I knew Trinidad to be unimportant, uncreative, cynical . . . skills were not required by a society which produced nothing, never had to prove its worth, and was never called upon to be efficient."[14] In fact, Caribbean history has produced "no people in the true sense of the word, with a character and purpose of their own. How can the history of this West Indian futility be written? . . . The history of these islands can never be satisfactorily told . . . History is built around achievement and creation; and nothing was created in the West Indies." Naipaul's latest work *The Loss of El Dorado* is surprisingly a historical treatise on Trinidad. It is a good book, but unfortunately at best Naipaul expresses a European concept of history. Wilson Harris has with great insight pointed to what has been wrong so far with both the detractors and defenders of Caribbean history. For Harris both are wrong in their approach to the writing of Caribbean history. He quotes from Gerald Moore's *The Chosen Tongue* "Both M. G. Smith . . . and V. S. Naipaul appear to believe that the West Indies possess no genuine inner cohesion whatever and no internal source of power. Having no common interests to cement them the inhabitants of the area can be held together only by external force. Professor Elsa Goveia reaches an opposite and equally depressing conclusion. She argues that the West Indies had one integrating factor historically, and this has been "the acceptance of the inferiority of the Negro to the white."[15] Harris then proceeds ". . . a cleavage exists . . . between the historical convention in the Caribbean and Guianas and the arts of the imagination. I believe a philosophy of history may lie buried in the arts of the imagination . . . Let us start with a myth stemming from Africa which has undergone metamorphosis. The one I have in mind is called limbo . . . They have no criteria for arts of originality springing out of any age of limbo and the history they write is without an inner time . . . Once we perceive this inner corrective to historical documentary and protest literature . . . we begin to participate (in) the genuine possibilities of original change in a people severley disadvantaged (it is true) at a certain point in time."[16] For the European oriented mind, history is tied to a linear line and is marked by the creation of something spatial. Authors who focused upon man-made utopia are a prominent feature of Western literature and thought. (Plato, More, Campanella, Bacon, Rousseau, Swift, Hawthorne, Huxley, Orwell, Skinner to name a few.) The enemy is movement and change. The time of man is linear and is measured against the chronos of the cosmos. Time is movement through space, and eternity is the elimination of movement, the confirmation of an everlasting present. Western man seeks the safety of the eternal and so advocates a timeless political space as man's material condition. Even God is subordinate to this temporally and ontologically prior cosmic order. (Re Plato's *Timaeus*.) Man is distinguished from God not by omnipotence but temporality. Man is the creature who not only dies, he also knows he will die. Hence, the postulated political space fixes on a—temporality, the construction of ordered space, the ideal city. The greatest art is the creation of utopia, the social cosmos, "the Empire on which the sun never sets." But Naipaul has lost faith in the ability of the Caribbean, and so he resorts to satire. In his most famous novel, *A House for Mr. Biswas*, Biswas sets out to build a house, the utopia. Most utopias are built on aesthetic mathematical principles, but naturally Biswas lacks a plan. Like the rejected artists in Plato's *The Republic*, he fails because he is concerned with appearance rather than forms. Hence, he builds a monstrosity. Naipaul cannot accept the Caribbean, because for them temporality becomes an escape from the bondage of political space e.g. Vodun, Pocomania. If they do speak of utopia it is not man made. It may lie in the future (Bedward) but if so it is transcendental, or it may lie in the past from which they are cut off by time (childhood or geography). Hence, a fair number of novels focus upon the transcendental—R. Mais *Brother Man*, S. Wynter *The Halls of Hebron*, A. Salkey *A Quality of Violence*, O. Patterson *The Children of Sisyphus*; childhood — M. Anthony *The Year in San Fernando*, A. Drayton *Christopher*, I. McDonald *The Humming Bird Tree*, G. Lamming *In the Castle of My Skin*; and journeys which reveal the non-existence of utopia — J. Carew, *The Last Barbarian, Moscow is not my Mecca*; A. Clarke, *The Meeting Point*; W. Collins, *Jamaican Migrant*; Hinds, *Journey to an Illusion*; G. Lamming, *The Emigrants*; O. Dathorne, *The Scholar Man*; A. Salkey, *Escape to an Autumn Pavement*; S. Selvon, *The Lonely Londoners, The Housing Lark*; D. Williams, *Other Leopards*. The most important work on the journey theme is Derek Walcott's *Dream on Monkey Mountain*. It is a major work and is the best play in English from the Caribbean.

Rhythm

This an old and familiar theme. Rhythm is an essential aspect of the culture of African people. But in neo African thought we can go further and can claim that *all art aspires to the state of music (rhythm)*. Janheinz Jahn in his book *Muntu and Neo African Literature* has consistently pointed out the rhythmical aspects of African cultures. "A poem, because it is written in English, does not necessarily belong to English poetry. We need only think of the difference between English and American literature to understand that . . . What enables us to draw the distinction is not the subject matter but the way in which it is treated; in a word, it is the style. Every culture . . . has its own characteristic manner or style which is displayed in its literature as in other things . . . I was trying to translate into German various African lyrics, some written in French, some in English and some in other languages . . . I tried to reproduce faithfully the music and rhythm of the language and as I went on I found that the phrasing had an entirely different melody and rhythm . . . There was such a striking similarity between the non-French and the non-English elements that it became clear that these were the purely African ones . . . When I went into the matter more closely, I found that this non European style came from the African poetic tridition."[17] Concerning style and rhythm, Leopold Senghor has this to say, "While modern Indo-Eurpean languages emphasize the abstract notion of time, African languages emphasize the *aspect,* the concrete way in which the action of the verb takes place . . . The image has no effect on the African unless it is rhythmical. Rhythm is consubstantial with the image . . .What is Rhythm? It is the architecture of being, the internal dynamic which confers form . . . the pure expression of the life force .. . Rhythm here does not arise from the alternation of long and short syllables but entirely from the alternation of stressed and unstressed syllables, strong beats and weak beats . . . a poem exists when stressed syllables recur after fixed intervals of time. But its essential rhythm is not that of speech but of the percussion instrument that accompanies the human voice, or rather those instruments that mark the basic rhythm . . . Music is related to speech and to dancing on the level of rhythm . . . In African music . . . the rhythm takes precedence over the melody. This is because the purpose of the music is less to please the ear than to re-enforce speech and make it more effctive. Hence, the place given to rhythm . . . the preference given to expression over harmony"[18] The importance of rhythm is quite evident in the music of the Blacks in the New World. Rhythm is also evident in the folk religions e.g. Vodun of Haiti, Pocomania of Jamaica, Shango of Trinidad. The evidence of rhythm in Caribbean literature is however not quite so obvious, because the language used, unless it is patois, is a European language. This language already reflects

Europe. The musician can express himself in an evident African mode because he is using a pure medium. This, of course, is why the African elements are so evident in the music. For neo African literature to be successful, it has to aspire to the state of music because (a)music is the dominant African art form (b) it is the art form which has most successfully survived the middle passage. Closely tied to this is the emphasis on rhythm over melody, and the place of improvisation. Up to quite recently Caribbean poetry has been an imitative art form, with the models coming from Europe. There were few outstanding poets. Claude McKay's works are distinguished from western poetry only by subject matter. The style and spirit is European, no wonder when England faced gloomy days in World War II after Dunkirk, Winston Churchill could rally the nation by reciting parts of McKay's most famous poem "If we must die". They must have been thankful for the poem of this 'anonymous' English poet. But McKay was very talented. The lesser poets during the thirties to the fifties confined themselves to writing about daffodils and other English romantic overtones. J. E. Claire McFarlane for a long time Jamaica poet laureate in his poem 'My Country' puts it this way "And I have sought, /Uneasy with the hidden pain, the woods/ On summer night, to listen to the leaves/ Whispering in solemn conclave." V. L. Virtue in 'The Web' is even more dainty, "Parting my window to the light/ That flooded up an April dawn,/ I beheld a vision bright / Upon a bough, across a lawn." At their most indigenous they might turn to the mango tree. V. L. Virtue "I have seen March" — "I have seen March within the Ebony break/ In golden fire of fragrance unsuppressed;/ And April bring the Lignum-Vitae dressed/ In dusty purple; known pale rust awake/ The Mango's bough."[19] This is all very sad. The first break came with the emergence of Derek Walcott. He is dazzling in his virtuosity, and he is breaking from the European obsession. His major works are *Selected Poems, The Castaways, The Gulf*. The second break came with Edward Brathwaite. He lived in Africa for eight years, and his present interest in Caribbean Folk culture has made possible the strongest and most original poetic voice. His trilogy *"Rights of Passage", "Masks"* and *"Islands"* is essentially neo African, the drums are there, but they are still struggling to take charge. Maybe in the near future they will. "I am a fuck-/ in' Negro,/ man, hole/ in my head,/ brains in/ my belly;/ black skin/ red eyes/ broad back/ big you know/ what." Yes, right on "Down down/ white/ man, con/ man, brown/ man/ . . . Rise rise/ locks-/ man, Solo-/ man wise/ man, rise/ rise rise." "So beat dem drums/ dem, spread / dem wings dem,/ watch dem fly/ dem, soar dem/ high dem."[20]

Time systems e.g. sasa and zamani are related. What constitutes one family of time as different from others is the *kind of units* which make it up, that is to say the character of the sasa, determining a series of similar sasa is distinguished from other kind of sasa which belong to other time systems. This implies that there are different kinds of present. Time is a complex entity built up of a plurality of temporal accents. Hence, in order to have a view of time as a whole one has to rise above the limits of one temporal stream and contemplate the relationship between different families of time. That is to say, one has to be capable of observing rhythm. Thus rhythm liberates one from a slavish confinement to a particular series of time. A rhythmical pattern, does not depend on the passage of events, because the events occur and vanish, whereas rhythm recurs and lasts. Not being obliterated along with the existential occurrences, rhythm may be called the memory of time. The beat of rhythm is different from the beat of everyday life. Everyday life is diluted by accidental and superfluous happenings. But this commonplace and ordinary existence is opposed to ritual and rhythm. Because time, not yet purified by rhythm, is often like a stammering man who repeats over and over again the same syllable and is incapable of proceeding farther. But in the shape of rhythm, time runs easily. Rhythmical phases are inter-related, because each rhythmical moment has a value not only in itself, but relatively to the whole pattern, thus the rhythmical scheme diverts attention from the dull tick of the mechanical time. Thus by means of rhythm one can anticipate, and so rhythm survives in a recurrence, because it leads the course of events. The variety of time systems is due to the variety of events which are constitutive in the formation of a time system. Hence, different events present different temporal units. When one kind of unit is selected and these units are connected in a sequence, a temporal rhythm is constructed which is different from other rhythms. It is this difference in rhythm which generates the different systems of time. In order to combine different units of time one must have recourse to a complex rhythmical pattern just as one combines different units of rhythm in poetry. And it is in relation to the pattern of rhythm that temporal factors may be estimated and qualified. Concerning *Masks,* Wilson Harris has this to say, "Take for example 'So the gods,/ masks of dreamers,/ hears lightnings/ stammer . . .' Note the echo of the drums, of thunder implied there is association with lightning that *stammers* across the sky.

That stammer — in association with the thunder of heaven's drum — constitutes the oracle of the poem . . . Edward Brathwaite is, I believe a Caribbean poet of renascence. He has been affected by African images but in an evolutionary way as I understand it."[21] It is of interest to note that Brathwaite has also written a number of critical articles in *Bim* (a Caribbean magazine originating from Barbados) 1967-8 entitled "Jazz and the West Indian Novel".

Homo Admirans v's Homo Faber

In neo African thought man lives in a sacramental universe. He is a creature who wonders. To wonder is to regard with reverence. The man of wonder is concerned with mystery. This approach to the world can be perverted in three ways: (a) The copying of a Wordsworthian approach to nature. The Caribbean intellectual is cut off from the folk, and so he tries to approach them through a European mind, all of this giving rise to imitation romantic poetry which I have dealt with above. (b) The attempt to separate Homo Admirans from Homo Faber, which dominated the school of Negritude. Aime Cesaire writes "Hurray for those who invented nothing/ for those who have never discovered/ for those who have never conquered/ but struck, deliver themselves to the essence of all things,/ ignorant of surfaces, but taken by the very movement of things/ not caring to conquer . . ."[22] The European is Homo Faber, he takes domination as his task, he dreams of ordered political space and the ideal city. But Cesaire has given too much away. When we say objects of wonder are mysterious we do not mean that they are vaguely known, mystery is not to be equated with the unknown or with ignorance. In fact, wonder is not anti-scientific. The mysteriousness of an object has little to do with how well or poorly it is known, and increase in knowledge does not necessarily lead to the decline of wonder. Writing on 'National Culture' in his book *The Wretched of the Earth,* Fanon has made other interesting objections to Negritude. At any rate the concept of Homo Admirans has been well developed by among others, George Lamming and Michael Anthony. Lamming's first novel *In the Castle of my Skin* is an excellent novel containing purple passages on Caribbean childhood. Since then Lamming has continued his exploration of Homo Admirans, but he has an unfortunate tendency to slip into the European romantic perspective. The exploration of the transcendental (mentioned above) is taken up by him in *Season of Adventure.* Unfortunately he has not published any novels since 1960. Anthony has the essential sensitivity, his novels are marked by a simple narrative style which allows for the evocation of mystery. (c) The disintegration of Homo Admirans into Homo Ludens. The contemporary Afro American novel teems with studies of Homo Ludens — Charles Wright: *The Wig;* Clarence Major: *All-Night Visitors;* Cecil Brown: *The Life and Loves of Mr. Jiveass Nigger.* Fanon attacks the disintegration of culture which manifests itself in tourism. "In its beginnings, the national bourgeoisie of the colonial countries identifies itself with the decadence of the bourgeoisie of the West . . . The national bourgeoisie will be greatly helped on its way toward decadence by the Western bourgeoisie, who come to it as tourists avid for the exotic, for big game hunting, and for casinos. The national bourgeoisie organizes centers of rest and relaxation and pleasure resorts to meet the wishes of the Western bourgoisie. Such activity is given the name of tourism, and for the occasion will be built up as a national industry"[23] Tourism has become the national industry of these islands, and with it goes the concept of Homo Ludens. The Caribbean becomes an entertainer, a dandy, above all a sexual athlete. Games become central to his life (one should be careful to separate play from games). Mais in his first novel *The Hills were Joyful Together* begins the exploration, and it has been developed by among others Selvon and Alvin Bennett.

Language

Above I referred to the relation between language and music, now I intend to explore the relation between language and Caribbean literature. The folk culture of the Caribbean is encased in a Sacramental Universe, comprised of a blending of Hebraic and African thought. The Bible plays a large part in the value system, and the speech patterns are affected in the English speaking territories by the King James Version, but above all those aspects of the Hebraic world view which corresponds to the African world view are absorbed into the folk culture. The colonizer as a European lives in a metaphysical system drawn from the Greeks (Christianity is more Hellenic than Hebraic. Note well that while Jesus must have spoken some type of Hebrew language, the New Testament was not written until several years [80 to 90!!] after his death and it was written in Greek, thus, there has been translation from one language to another, from one metaphysical system to another. Since that time a body of doctrine built around Greek philosophy has shrouded the entire interpretation of the Bible). The Colonized approaches the Bible with a metaphysical system drawn from Africa, India, etc. Hebraic thinking is dynamic, this is somewhat modified by the translation into English or into Greek and then into English. But the dynamism is restored in the Caribbean folk world because the African world is also dynamic. "Christian thought in the West . . . Its metaphysics has most generally been based upon a fundamental static conception of being. Herein is to be seen the fundamental difference between Western thought and that of the Bantu . . . We (the European) hold a static conception of "being", they a dynamic, the concept "force" is bound to the concept "being" . . . Force is even more than a necessary attribute of being: Force is the nature of being, force is being, being is force . . . In contradistinction to our definition of being as "that which is" or "the thing insofar as it is", the Bantu definition reads "that which is force."[24] This difference is to some extent mirrored by the Greek, Hebraic schism. Greek "to be" expresses existence or acts as a copula. Hebrew often drops the copula and so does Creole speech. "Linguistic forms, such as the absence of copula (he sick) . . . these forms of the "Negro" dialect can be related to analogous forms in say, Sranan and Saramaccan (Creole languages in Surinam) where they belong to stable internally coherent language systems"[25] Identity is established without the copula. To be in Creole speech means more than to exist or to become, it is active and can effect. Two material factors operate in man's cognitive relation to the environment. (a) Our language, thought and perception are shaped to some extent by the practical demands of survival and successful adaptation to the environment. (b) Language in its turn exerts important influences on our thought and perception. Language functions as a screen which classifies and selects experiences, for the purpose of responding to the environment. Hence, by its structural language significantly determines our experiences. Language has two functions: (a) It is a device for reporting experiences (b) More significantly it is a way of defining experience. So that, our world is to a large extent built upon the language habits of our linguistic group. Language shapes the cognition of the user. Different languages produce different cognitive structures. Hence, different linguistic communities perceive and conceive reality differently. The Caribbean writer is faced with an enormous problem. The educational system is European, the language is English. Until quite recently the books were published in England or the U.S.A. and his audience was overwhelmingly foreign. In order to get the book published or to survive financially he has to write so that the English speaking outsider can understand. This review in Bim of *"Syrop"* by Garth St. Omer illustrates the problem. "Syrop must have been written about 1957. I remember seeing it in typescript. My only regret is that it appears that in seeking a publisher, St. Omer has had to remove . . . the marvellous mixture and flavour of French creole speech and English narrative from the story, and provide instead what amounts to a translation of the creole."[26] The colonial situation, his western education, the extent and depth of the receptivity of the North Atlantic audience, all these factors determine the orientation of his writing. Claude McKay did write verse in dialect. But the real beginning to the usage of Creole speech patterns in the literature was Victor Reid's *New Day* 1949. I said 'speech patterns' because Reid did not get beyond that to the essential nature of Creole thought. Samuel Selvon makes a greater effort. His novels are quite a contrast to those of Naipaul. Naipaul thinks in standard English and then transliterates certain sections to Creole, while Selvon thinks in Creole and then transliterates certain sections into standard English. But, the problem has not been solved. Wilson Harris does major explorations in language but his interest lies outside the English-Creole conflict. Garth St. Omer and Lindsay Barrett have produced interesting experiments. (Of the new novelists Barrett's *Song for Mumu* is in my opinion the major talent.)

V. S. Naipaul

"It was not long after that Ganesh saw a big new notice in the shop, painted on cardboard.

'Is Leela self who write that,' Ramlogan said. 'I didn't ask she to write it, mind you. She just sit down quiet quiet one morning after tea and write it off.'

It read:

NOTICE!

NOTICE, IS, HEREBY: PROVIDED: THAT, SEATS! ARE, PROVIDED. FOR: FEMALE: SHOP, ASSISTANTS!

Ganesh said, 'Leela know a lot of punctuation marks.'

'That is it, sahib. All day the girl just sitting down and talking about these punctuation marks. She is like that, sahib.'[27]

When Leela leaves Ganesh her note reads,

"I, cannot; live: here, and, put; up: with, the, insult; of: my. Family!"[28]

These quotes are rather typical of Naipaul's early works. Like Marshall McLuhan he is interested in the impact of communication technology on culture. For McLuhan the underlying cause of social and cultural change is technological innovations of communication. The things by or through which words are transmitted are more important than the words themselves. Hence the medium is the message. Modes of communication are devices for fixing and organizing experience. They have built into them a grammar of logic for organizing experience and the grammar is found in the particular ratio of sensory qualities. While McLuhan is interested in tracing the impact which the shift from audile-tactile to visual-print and then to the electronic media have caused on a world wide basis, Naipaul in his early novels, focuses on the impact of visual-print upon the audile-tactile oriented people of Trinidad. This divide for Naipaul is also the divide between the universal man and the contemptible strivers. While McLuhan admires the virtues of the audile-tactile world, Naipaul is so trapped in the visual-print world, so convinced of its superiority that to him the audile-tactile world is inferior, and the audile-tactile people can at best be comical strivers trying to enter into the glory of the visual-print universe. This is the source of his early comic novels, and at the same time his weakness. He lacks all comprehension of the virtues of the audile-tactile world. Naipaul is intent on making fun of those in transition, as if to say they are stupid or that they are unique in this situation. But this situation has often been repeated historically, and in fact the pre print era of Western culture included the civilizations of Ancient Israel, Greece and Rome, and such personalities as Jesus, Plato, Aristotle, St. Augustine. Print depends on phonetic writing, and phonetic writing translates the oral into the visual, translates sound into visual symbols. Besides making us dependent upon the eye, print imposes a particular logic on the organization of our experiences. Print breaks up and organizes reality into elementary units, forcing us to see reality as discrete units, to perceive events in linear serial order and to find an orderly structure in things. The visual arrangement of the printed page becomes the perceptual model by which all experience is organized. Now it is true that the person in transition from the auditory to the print world encounters punctuation, spelling, etc., as a problem; but the model Naipaul presents is a misrepresentation because he is not presenting the figure in transition, but rather Naipaul the bright print entrapped individual projects the extreme theoretical absurdities of his own medium upon those who are trying to come to terms with that medium. In other words the peculiar posters and signs, the unusual mistakes in punctuation and grammar are not the product of Naipaul's characters, but of brilliant people like Naipaul who although they have fully mastered the world of the colonizer still feel uneasy, are always in dread of the theoretical absurd, the slip of the tongue, etc., and who diminish their fear by projecting in magnified form, extreme theoretical absurdities and logical flaws of the print culture on all those e.g. the colonial world, who trigger their fears. McLuhan points out that no one made grammatical errors in non-literate society, and the obsession with errors in spelling and punctuation only arose with the print. But if McLuhan is correct the greatest absurdity of all is that the electronic media have now replaced the visual-print media, and Naipaul's unease may in fact be due to his unconscious realization that the world he strove so hard to enter is crumbling fast, and in fact began to crumble even before he published his first book. (Television was already making its impact when Naipaul published his first book in 1957. His style interesting enough remains quite Victorian.)

Sociological and Political Overtones

Sociology and Politics have been the chief concern of the Caribbean novelists and have caused most of the major failures. Most of the novelists are middle class Western educated intellectuals who see the Caribbean social world from the perspective of liberal left-wing oriented humanities text books. This blunted Claude McKay's presentation. Mittelholzer tried everything. He wrote historical novels *(The Kaywana Series),* thrillers and mysteries *(The Weather in Middenshot, My Bones and My Flute, Eltonsbrody),* novels based on literary experiments motivated by Wagner's lietmotive techniques *(Latticed Echoes, Thunder Returning),* novels probing ethnic relations and perversions *(A Morning at the Office, Shadows Move Among Them; Life and Death of Sylvia, the Piling of Clouds, Uncle Paul),* and novels examining suicide *(The Wounded and the Worried, the Jilkinson Drama).* Mittelholzer committed suicide. But he had committed suicide long before that — cultural suicide. John Hearne lacks the pungency of Mittelholzer. He is uneasy in the Caribbean world and this is sublimated in his novels, a good example of which is the imaginary island Cayuna in which his later novels are set. Why bother, Cayuna is a mirror image of Jamaica. Hearne and his characters are obsessed with escaping — from themselves, and their surroundings and yet their flight is evanescent. Of late, with the aid of Morris Cargill he has turned to the thriller-detective format, leaving us with one good novel, his first, *Voices Under the Window.* J. Carew, *Black Midas, The Wild Coast;* A. Clarke, *The Survivors of the Crossing, Amongst Thistles and Thorns;* N. Dawes, *The Last Enchantment;* M. Ferguson, *Village of Love;* F. Frazer, *Wounds in the Flesh;* F. Hercules, *Where the Humming-Bird Flies;* I. Khan, *Jumbie Bird;* Peter Kempadoo, *Guyana Boy, Old Thom's Harvest;* E. Lovelace, *While Gods Were Falling, The Schoolmaster;*

S. Naipaul, *Firefles;* V. S. Naipaul, *The Mystic Masseur, The Suffrage of Elvira, Miguel Street, A House for Mr. Biswas, The Mimic Men;* A. Salkey, *The Late Emancipation of Jerry Stover, The Adventures of Catullus Kelly;* G. St. Omar, *A Room on the Hill, Shades of Grey, Nor Any Country,* have all placed their emphasis on sociological and political explorations. The explorations are essential for any developing country or area, but in several cases these explorations fail. It is not the topic which caused these failures (although one must admit that it is the most difficult in literature to deal with), rather it is the orientation. What I have said above about history and time also holds true for sociology and politics. The orientation is wrong.

FOOTNOTES

1. Harris, W.—"History, Fables and Myth in the Caribbean and Guianas"—*Caribbean Quarterly* Vol. 16 No. 2. June 1970, p. 25
2. I shall use the word 'Caribbean' to refer to the non European population of the Caribbean area
3. Mbiti, J. S.—*African religions and philosophy*—London: Heinemann, 1969, p. 257
4. Mbiti, pp. 17-19
5. Reid, V.—*New Day;* N. Y. Knopf 1949, p. 18
6. Reid, p. 361
7. Reid, pp. 362-4
8. Eccles 3: 1-8
9. Harris, W.—*Palace of the Peacock;* London: Faber 1960, p. 37
10. Harris, "History, Fable and Myth" p. 28
11. Harris, "History, Fable and Myth" p .28
12. Harris, "History, Fable and Myth" pp. 13-14. See also his other works, *The Far Journey of Dudin, The Whole Armour, The Secret Ladder, Heartland, The Eye of the Scarecrow, The Waiting Room, Tumatumari,* and *Ascent to Omai.*
13. Harris, "History, Fable and Myth" p. 24
14. Naipaul, V. S.—*"The Middle Passage";* London: Deutsch 1962, pp. 41-42
15. More, G. — *"The Chosen Tongue";* London: Longmans 1969, p. 67
16. Harris, "History, Fable and Myth" pp. 6-10
17. Jahn, J. — Rhythm and Style in African Poetry, in *"African Literature and the University";* edited by G. Moore Ibaden U.P. 1965, pp. 51, 53
18. Senghor, L. — *Prose and Poetry;* London: Oxford U.P. 1965, pp. 84-89
19. See the following collections:
Anthology of W. I. Poetry (ed. A. J. Seymour) *Kykoveral* No. 22, 1957
Anthology of W. I. Poetry, *Caribbean Quarterly* Vol 5 No. 3, 1958
Independence Anthology of Jamaican Literature Jamaica: The Ministry of Development and Welfare, 1962
20. Brathwaite, E.—*Rights of Passage;* London: Oxford 1967, pp. 29, 42-43
21. Harris, W. —"History, Fable and Myth" p. 24
22. Cesaire, A.—*Return to my Native Land;* Paris: Presence Africaine, 1969, pp. 101-102

23. Fanon, F. — *The Wretched of the Earth*; N. Y.: Grove Press, 1968, p. 153
24. Temples, P. — *Bantu Philosophy;* Paris: Presence Africaine, 1969, pp. 50-52
25. Alleyne, M. C. — "The Linguistic Continuity of Africa in the Caribbean; *Black Academy Review,* Vol. 1 No. 4, p. 7
26. Bim 40, pp. 290-291
27. V. S. Naipaul, *The Mystic Masseur*; London: Penguin, pp. 43-44
28. Naipaul, p. 88

THE CALYPSO TRADITION
IN WEST INDIAN LITERATURE
by
Lloyd W. Brown

The American novelist, Clarence Farmer, recently ridiculed the "awful" calypso tunes of the West Indies, particularly those "happey-darkey Banana Boat songs and Brown-Skinned Girls" which Harry Belafonte popularized in North America.[1] There is some justification for an attack on the erotic inanities which have been profitably marketed in North America as "calypsoes." But we need to question the assumption that these are representative of a genuine calypso tradition indigenous to the West Indies, and that the "happey-darkey" image of the Black Sambo stereotype pertains to the authentic calypso as well as to Belafonte's ersatz offerings. For in truth both the outside critic and the uninformed imitator run the risk of perceiving the calypsonian and his art in superficial terms. They may be pre-occupied with a "happy" and carefree style, to the exclusion of the song's cultural and moral significance. Or, like Clarence Farmer, they may leap to the conclusion that the calypso simply perpetuates the old subhuman image of joyous darkies singing "simple and simple-minded music," with the usual hand-clapping, mindless, teeth-displaying, sweat-rolling, shoulder-shaking" (*Soul On Fire*, p. 111).

But, curiously, these are precisely the kinds of misconception which have bedeviled an understanding of the Black American's own poetry and music: the comic style and rhythms of his art have been accepted at face value rather than as the ironic presentation of the tragic and the near tragic. In the 1890's the Black poet Paul Dunbar explores the protective deceptiveness which characterizes the Black experience:

> We wear the mask that grins and lies,
> It hides our cheeks and shades our eyes,—
> This debt we pay to human guile;
> With torn and bleeding hearts we smile,
> And mouth with myriad subtleties.

This is the grinning mask that has misled the outside world: "let them only see us, while / We wear the mask."[2] More recently, Ralph Ellison examines the "near-cominc" mask of the blues tradition in Black America: "The blues is an impulse to keep the painful details and episodes of a brutal experience alive in one's aching consciousness, to finger its jagged grain, and to transcend it, not by the consolation of philosophy but by squeezing from it a near-tragic, near-comic lyricism. As a form, the blues is an autobiographical chronicle of personal catastrophe expressed lyrically." Thus in a Bessie Smith song the lyrical prose "evokes the paradoxical, almost surreal image of a black boy singing lustily as he probes his own grievous wound.[3]

Ellison's thesis is echoed in the Caribbean by the Barbadian poet, Edward Brathwaite, *apropos* of Caribbean work songs. For the latter sees the West Indian's laughter and song as a defensive reflex which is rooted in, and masks, the pain of Black history:

> Drum skin whip
> lash, master sun's
> cutting edge of
> heat, taut
> surfaces of things
> I sing
> I shout
> I groan
> I dream.[4]

Braithwaite explains the function of laughter and music in the West Indian experience in terms which are not dissimilar to the grinning mask of Paul Dunbar's Black Americans. The exuberant rhythms and shouts of the Caribbean work song are inseparable from the suffering that necessitated them in the first place. The West Indian's laughter is a defensive disguise for suffering. Simultaneously, it is a means of attack, for according to another Barbadian, the novelist George Lemming, "West Indians are in the habit of laughing at every goddam thing."[5] And this is the mask which the Calypsonian employs, both as composer and singer, when he transforms the "happey-darkey" image into a stalking-horse for trenchant satire, or into an ironic technique which juxtaposes the "near-tragic" and the "near-comic."

The West Indian writer has been quick to exploit the satiric ambiguities inherent in the calypso tradition. Thus Paule Marshall who is an American of Barbadian parentage draws upon the calypso's satiric form in her *Brown Girl Brownstones* (1959), a novel on the West Indian community in Brooklyn. When Deighton Boyce scandalizes his friends by squandering the family savings, the calypso automatically becomes the community's ritualistic weapon of expulsion: "From all over the hall those dark contemptuous faces charged him. Those eyes condemned him and their voices rushed full tilt at him, scourging him and finally driving him from their presence with their song, 'Small Island, go back where you really come from!'"[6] The dance and the song are a convivial mask for satire: they dramatize and represent the outraged solidarity which forever excludes Deighton from their midst. But, simultaneously, these festive gestures are a comic disguise for the pain which the dancers share communally with Deighton's victimized family.

This calypsonian irony is also exemplified by Edward Brathwaite's poetic analysis of Caribbean folk music: the poem's burden of pain and sorrow ("skin whip/lash . . . I groan") is disguised by the pulsating drum-rhythms of "I sing/ I shout/ I groan/ I dream." Hence the central line of the passage, "surface of things," literally becomes the pivot of the poet's irony. The surface of the exuberant drum is juxtaposed with the skin of the whipped slave to become twin symbols of triumphant song-in-suffering. But the phrase both mocks and warns the unwary or the uninitiated who respond superficially to the pleasing "surfaces of things" in the West Indian's music and life-style — without perceiving the palpable realities which have historically been symbolized by the skin of slave and drum. And this is the warning which another West Indian poet, Derek Walcott of St. Lucia, issues to the outsider, to the "brassy visitor from the hard cities," who confuses titillating tourist posters with the Caribbean reality: "O warn him, Terror, of contagions he knows well,/ That we who seem unreal are only willing/ To accept the glamour as a firce background to sorrow."[7]

The West Indian writer's interest in what I have represented here as calypsonian irony is not really surprising. A poet like Edward Brathwaite, for example, emphasizes that the calypsonian's materials and skills are indispensable to the poet's art: the calypso "may help the Indian poet to realize the rhythmic organisation which our poets have not yet discovered — or if they have, have not yet exploited." Indeed, the calypsonian *is* an artist in his own right, and critics are mistaken when they start off "with the preconception that an artist like Sparrow is in some way an entirely different being from an artist, say, like myself or Derek [Walcott] or any of the others."[8] As we shall see in due course, a limited number of West Indian writers do exploit the "rhythmic organisation" which the calypsonian derives from West Indian dialects. But despite the general short-comings in this regard, it is clear that Brathwaite, Marshall, and others have more than passing interest in the ironic techniques of the calypsonian artist. And of these artists the most successful is "Sparrow," — "Slinger" Francisco of Grenada (now residing in Trinidad).

Like most calypso singers and writers, Sparrow has a wide repertoire: sexual intrigue, politics, poverty, racism, and all the ingredients of everyday life in the West Indian village. The polymetric structure of most songs, their seemingly "trivial" topics, and the steady rhythm of the musical background all combine to suggest a light-hearted exercise in the banal and the erotic.[9] Sparrow's description of the traditional lover's plea in "Lulu" is typical:

> You makin' skylark, Lulu
> I am surprised at you
> I give you my word of honour
> I want you to remember
> I won't mention a word to anyone
> What is done is done
> Don't destroy my heart like a Christmas toy
> Let's spread some joy.
> > Ah'm afraid you make a calypso o' me
> > Ah know nobody goin see, an' is only the two o' we
> > Sparrow Ah 'fraid you goin' make a calypso o' me.

Sparrow's mockery of his "coy" mistress' hypocrisy is clear. Her sexual "morality" is based on public reputation rather than on principle. The sensual instinct to "spread joy" is countered by the fear of the calypsonian's notorious practice of converting private or public lives into an object of ridicule. But looked at closely, the song is more than an erotic plea for free love. It is also a serious examination of the calypsonian's function in society. More precisely, Sparrow appears to question the painful, sometimes brutal process, through which the calypsonian fulfils his role as political commentator, satirist, and social critic. The calypsonian's "word of honour," like Lulu's chastity, may be fragile, even imaginary. And like the more conventional journalist whose shoes he often occupies, the calypsonian is in constant danger of blurring the faint line between the "honour" of fair criticism, and the banal obscenities of mere scandal-mongering. In effect, the bawdy style and the highly conventional situation disguise the double-edged irony with which Sparrow develops his themes of social criticism and artistic self-scrutiny: the double standards and hypocrisy of "public" morality are juxtaposed with the moral ambiguity of satire in general, and of the calypso in particular. The "grinning mask" of the carefree lecher becomes a medium for the calypsonian's self-appraisal.

This is the kind of lecherous calypsonian mask that Ismith Khan (Trinidad) exploits in *The Obeah Man* (1964), a novel set in Trinidad's carnival season. The calypso and its accompanying steel band are the essence of the exuberant carnival spirit:

> The steel drums and the other musicians had started playing, only slowly now as though each player was seeking out the core of the music, looking for the essence of its meaning before they would burst forth in unison with the calypso of this carnival, and the melody, the rhythm, the emotion of flesh meeting flesh was being probed by the music like hungry fingers in search of the right key to open the door to explosion.
> 'Iron something bend up my something
> Oh . . . Man — Man — Ti — Re!
> Iron something bust up my nothing
> Oh . . . Man — Man — Ti — Re![10]

The erotic excitement of the song and its musical accompaniment is intensified when Zolda, one of the carnival celebrants, dances in public; for her unabashed sexuality complements the calypso's phallic symbolism (pp. 52-53). And the sexual images of dancer and song are reinforced by the tell-tale masks and floats of the carnival parade — devils, dragons, and "U.S.S. Bad Behavior" — by the animalistic atmosphere of the annual "fete," and by "the full spirit of the bacchanal, the savage and profane humour of carnival" (p. 6).

But like Sparrow's "Lulu," Khan's novel uses the calypsonian image of the animalistic lecher to explore the moral and emotional ambiguities of calypso and the calypsonian's society (represented in *Obeah Man* by the carnival as a social microcosm). For Khan's work is an analysis of deep-seated emotional and cultural crises which lie beneath the attitudinal and physical masks of carnival time. Indeed, there is actually an unmasking scene in the novel when one of the dancers has his disguise removed — and the findings are significant: "the Beast's mask was ugly, grinning, and vicious, yet inside that front was an exhausted man . . . under the grotesque mask was the man's face, covered with sweat; tears rolling down the fold of his cheeks, then he started sobbing like a child" (p. 134). Hence the tears beneath the dancer's grinning front are comparable with the cultural ironies which Paul Dunbar attributes to the Black American's life-style, which Ellison sees as the dynamic of the blues, and which Brathwaite exemplifies in his poetic critique of the West Indian's folk culture. The vitality, even the exuberant animalism, of the calypso-carnival in Khan's novel emerges as the facade of the West Indian reality. Within this ambiguous context, the phallic connotations of "Iron something bust up my nothing" quickly become a grim reminder of hard times, of the "iron" reality of having "nothing."

In part, the paradox of laughter in pain, ecstacy in agony, is a universal human faculty: "The human body is savage . . . it is saint. It cries out for vast varieties of sensations . . . It weeps at sunrise on beholding a crystal dewdrop balancing in the hammock of a spider's web, then plunges limb and bone into a savage pounding of feet to drums and music, writhing, sweating in an ecstacy that is at once a punishment" (p. 49). But the lust for life and laughter, as antidotes to death and suffering, has always been especially strong in the tropics where history has, ironically, combined the beauty and fertility of the environment with the ugliness and destructiveness of slavery and colonialism. It is against this background of cruel, historical paradoxes that we must view what Khan calls the "desperate bid for life in the tropics" — with regards to both men and nature: "The long-tongued lashes of the sea lap upon the edges of the earth as if waiting a chance to swallow the island — the sun rushes into men's bones igniting them like fireworks, rushing on their slow flicker into a quick burst of flame, hurrying them on to their cinder-bed" (p. 104). So that to ignore the West Indian paradox of beauty in ugliness, life in death, is to miss the hidden meanings of the laughter, songs, and dances in the calypso-carnival. And this error, so similar to the superficial judgements of Paul Dunbar's White American outsiders and Derek Walcott's "brassy" tourists, is perpetuated by another tourist in Khan's novel. For, according to Zampi, the obeah man, the White visitor is incapable of seeing beyond the beautiful scenery and smiling faces of the island: "Man! you fellers don't know how lucky you are. All you have to do is put your hand outside your window, pick your banana and grapefruits off a tree, have breakfast, and go back to sleep" (p. 66). Yet if the dancer's tears are easily exposed by looking beneath his mask, it is also simple for the discerning and the sensitive to appreciate the actuality behind the island's natural beauty. Hence Zampi reminds the carnival revellers that despite the joyous bacchanal, they are all the "dead" inhabitants of a blighted and moribund world which had been exploited and then abandoned: "You dead, and I dead . . . The people who put up all them buildings, them big big churches with clock to tell time by . . . they dead and gone. They did plan to stay and they build them things to last for ever, but Trinidad blight" (p. 66).

Finally, the symbolic paradox of the grinning mask dominates personal conflicts which are intensified by the calypso-carnival. Zolda's erotic response to the calypso theme-song, "Man — Man — Ti — Re," dramatizes an irrepressible vitalism and a passionate affirmation of sex as a life-force: "as she arched still farther back, the sailor pants drawn like the skin of a drum over her thighs, her breasts slipped backwards so that now the pale light brown of her skin . . . could be seen." But the dance is akin to the life-death, beauty-ugliness, and laughter-pain antitheses which the mask symbolizes in personal relationships in the novel. For Zolda is partnered by Hop-and-Drop, an embittered and vicious cripple who is hypersensitive about his undeveloped manhood and whose dancing is as grotesque as his figure. And to multiply his ironic links with Zolda, the life-force, the clacking sounds of Hop-and-Drop's dance-steps conjure up a picture of drum-sticks — thereby completing the image which began with the drum-skin reference to Zolda's thighs: "the cripple danced out to her, his one foot stomping, the other clacking" (pp. 52, 53). On the other hand, Massahood, another of Zolda's admirers, is the epitome of physical manhood: "His body and his bones were made for love, women smelt it from his nostrils, tasted it from his mouth, and knew it in that amorphous way that animals in heat single out each other" (p. 56). Massahood's bestial masculinity incarnates the lecher-image of the calypso mask and the bacchanalian spirit of the carnival as a whole. But he, too, has a counterpart: Zampi, Zolda's estranged lover, who has renounced the carnival in order to become an obeah man — a religious mystic and medicine-man. In effect, Massahood's limited definitions of manhood ("massahood") cripples him by confining him to the physical *surfaces* of the carnival experiences. And it is significant that as competitors for Zolda's favors, both himself and that other cripple, Hop-and-Drop, die violently — the former being stoned to death by a mob after he had murdered his rival.

The deaths which conclude the carnival demonstrate, climactically, the conflicts and paradoxes represented by the calypso mask. The double tragedy confronts Zolda with the realities which are usually disguised by the desperate conviviality of the carnival season: "All the moments of pleasure she knew, all the recklessness that drove her, left her now, and she felt as though she were in an empty house where all manner of debauchery had been acted out, leaving behind only the dirty confetti, the flat limp streamers that she, Zolda, was now left to tidy up, to be haunted by the emptiness, the hollowness, the sight of the two dead men. In her own way she saw now what Zampi must have felt, she could understand why he had taken himself away" (p. 186). Altogether, Zolda's penetration of physical appearances around her fulfils the symbolic prediction inherent in Zampi's removal of the Beast mask from the tired dancer. And both forms of unmasking, the physical and the perceptual, are, significantly, presented in the calypso-carnival context. They demonstrate the parallels between Khan the novelist and Sparrow the calypsonian, for both artists are using the "Beast" mask of the lecher in order to project equally ironic insights into the paradoxes of the West Indian experience.

Sparrow's "Congo Man" is a fair example of the manner in which the grinning Beast mask is used deliberately to assume a subhuman role which has, historically, been assigned by the White outsider. Thus at a superficial glance, the song appears to be a sympathetic expression of the Westerner's contempt for African "savages" in the "dark" continent:

> Two White women travellin' through Africa
> Fin' themselves in the hands of a cannibal head-hunter
> He cook up one an' he eat one raw
> They tas'e so good he wanted more
> Mo - o - o re!
> Ah! he want more!
>
>> I envy the Congo Man
>> I wish I coulda go an' shake he han'
>> He eat until he stomach upset,
>> An' I . . . I never eat a white meat yet!
>> Ho! ha! ha! hoo!

And when the repeated "white meat" references make the (interracial) sexual motif unmistakable, it could seem at first that Sparrow has merely reproduced the stereotype of the white goddess's Black stud:

> Peepin' through the bushes to see what's takin' place
> There I saw the Congo Man goin' t otake a tas'e
> He close he eyes, he start to grin
> Rubbin' he belly he mumblin'
> Ha! ha! ha! he! he! he!

> I envy the Congo Man (etc.)
> One of the women started to beg
> He bite she on the ches' he bite she on the leg.
> Ha! ha! ha! hee! hee! haw!
> Aye! aye! aye!

But it is really difficult to miss the satiric implications of laughter in the song, especially when the singer reproduces and mocks the Congo Man's bestial, and expectant, chuckles: "An' when the water was warm she started to wiggle/ The Congo Man started to laugh an' giggle/ Ha! ha! ha! kla kla! kla!" For the sheer exaggeration of the singer's laughter is suggestive. The Congo Man is an object of ridicule, not as an African reality, but as the image which White Westerners have about Africans and other Blacks: Africans are savages, and all Black men have an insatiable, bestial appetite for White women. Hence the song's laughter becomes an important satiric weapon that is typical of the calypsonian's irony. The animal sounds of expectation reproduce White myths about Black sexuality. But the exaggeration deliberately invokes the horrific, and in so doing, the singer recreates the atmosphere of paranoia, the nightmarish sense of insecurity, which encourage White fantasies about the Black stud. Moreover, Sparrow's irony is directed at the victims of the White man's psycho-sevual myths — at the White woman who accepts the myth of Black super-sexuality, and at the Black man who is obsessed with the image of White femininity. Thus the Congo Man's stereotypical role becomes a paradigm of the singer's own desires ("I envy the Congo Man"). And the Black man's desire-hate for the White woman, as an object of sexual craving and racial "revenge," is dramatized by the sadistic fulfillment implied by the cannibal motif. On her side, the White woman's loathing for, and fear of, the savage cannibal simply reinforces a masochistic yearning for the forbidden. Apparent resistance ("wiggle") and cries of supplication ("beg") actually become forms of excited compliance.

Of course these fantasies about miscegnation have been extensively analysed.[11] But it is significant that when a West Indian novelist like Austin Clark (Barbados) turns to this theme he bases his approach on the ironic structure of the calypso — including the satiric viewpoint of Sparrow's song. Thus in *The Meeting Point* (1967) the sexual tensions at an interracial party in Toronto, Canada, develop against the musical background of a calypso song. Two West Indians, Boysie and Henry, cavort with White girls and neglect Black women, including Boysie's wife Dots, and their hostess, Bernice Leach. And in this setting, a Sparrow calypso in praise of Black virility provides an appropriate background: "I ain't boasting, but I know I got durability . . . if a woman ever tell you that I ever left her dis-satisfy, she lie! she lie! she lie!"[12] As in his "Congo Man," Sparrow's crude image of the Black stud is ironic here. Thus Clark uses the calypso to create a *mythic* illusion, a mask, a Black virility, which shapes the stereotypical patterns of the Black man's behavior and the expectant co-operation of his White partner. However, beneath this illusion there is the emotional and moral fragility which counteracts Boysie's, and Henry's claims to durable manhood. Boysie is unemployed, and is supported by a wife whom he loathes; while Henry, an unemployed railroad porter, has long been reduced to fantasizing about large bank accounts and real estate holdings. Moreover, their obsession with White women disqualify them from that really durable manhood which is rooted in racial pride, in "Blackhood." Sparrow's indictment of this self-betrayal is very pertinent here, for Clarke pointedly paraphrases a line from the "Congo Man" to which the mixed couples dance at a later point in the party: "Sparrow was asking his audience, in song, whether they . . . had ever tasted a 'white beef (sic) yet' " (p. 71).

Finally, Clarke's ironic implications are multiplied by the ambivalence of the Black women themselves toward Black masculinity. Bernice is comparable with Sparrow's *voyeur* in "Congo Man." She is repelled by the Black man's slavering obsession with White women; but, simultaneously, she is envious of her White rivals and fascinated with the Black man's sexuality. Boysie's "gyrations" on the dance floor please her: she urges him, in her thoughts, to humiliate the White Brigette — in dancing and in bed. This urging is not only in response to her own unfulfilled sexual desires: it is also a vicarious form of that familiar gambit in the Black experience — sexual "revenge" against Whites. And in this case, Bernice's "victims" are not only the interloping White girls at her party, but also the White man, that perennial desecrator of Black womanhood who seems, of late, to be sizing up her plump figure through the eyes of her employer, Mr. Burrmann (p. 72). In short, Clarke has reproduced the double-edged irony of Sparrow's calypso songs: the images of Black masculinity are presented with self-flattering masks which are torn apart in the very moment that they are used, ironically, to tittilate both the artist's characters and his audience.

The calypsonian's mask may also be allowed to slip gradually. And in a song like "Maria," Sparrow's irony is centered on the stage-by-stage exposure of an idealized mistress who turns out to be a heart-breaking two-timer. Hence his persona's language and perception progress from trite, romantic cliches to painful reality. He begins with the usual, time-worn declarations of love:

> Maria darling I must go
> But remember I love you so.
> Well unfortunately we must part,
> Girl you don't know how it breaks my heart.
> I wish I could stay with you
> And give you what is yours to do.
> O-o-o-o-o-o-o-o-h Maria-a-a!

But "love" turns out to be an exclusively physical commodity for which Maria's "idealistic" admirer is prepared to barter in hard cash:

> I like the way you walk, Marie,
> An' I like the way you talk, Marie.
> I like the way you smile, Marie
> It's very easy to see Marie
> How much you mean to me Marie.
> I don't care if I starve Marie
> You'll get all the money I have Marie.

And this gradual exposure of Sparrow's persona for what he really is foreshadows and complements the final revelations about Maria herself. There is also a corresponding shift in style. Under the pressure of real, rather than assumed, emotion, there is less emphasis on the pretentious formalities of "good" English. The shift from the orthodox "I" to the dialect "Ah" from "my" to "me" is partly a vocal subtlety, but it is highly suggestive nonetheless:

> Ah went home to Marie las' night
> But someone nearly out me light;
> Ah don't know his reas'n
> But the police have him in pris'n;
> Ah don't know if what he said was true
> He says he love Maria too.
> So now Ah can't see what to do,
> Because he has my eyes black 'n' blue.

On the whole, what promises to be a trite "complaint" about the unfaithful mistress turns out to be a gradual expansion of ironic insights. The lover's expose of Maria's infidelity quickly becomes the occasion for his own inadvertent self-betrayal. And even beyond this, the individual hypocrisies of the two lovers are linked to the wider connotations of the cultural and emotional significance of language. For there seems to be an important link between pretense and the more formal style of the earlier stanzas, and, on the other hand, between sincerity and dialect forms in the closing verse. These equations are culturally symbolic. They reflect the West Indian artist's traditional assumptions about the ethnological significance of dialect, as distinct from "orthodox" English. The latter is the emblem of the metropolitan power and of the West Indian's status as a colonial or ex-colonial. On the other hand, his "real" roots are to be found in the unassimilated peasantry whose dialect embodies those Afro-West Indian traditions which have not been destroyed or diluted by the "White" middle-class values of Western education. The cultural assumptions which inform the closing stanza of Sparrow's "Maria" are therefore important to West Indian novelists like George Lamming. According to the latter, the West Indian writer differs from his English counterpart because the West Indian is "essentially peasant." He has never left the land that once claimed their ancestors like trees. His prose is "the people's speech, the organic music of the earth . . . For soil is a large part of what the West Indian has brought back to reading; lumps of earth: unrefined, perhaps, but good, warm, fertile earth" (*The Pleasures of Exile,* pp. 45-46).

This is the soil which Derek Walcott explores in "Tales of the Islands" where the carnival "fete" is described from two perspectives. First, it is seen through the condescending viewpoint of an Oxbridge (Oxford and Cambridge) graduate, with the usual notions of "savages" and with the tell-tale correctness of "cultured" speech. Then Walcott switches to the peasant's point of view which mocks the shallow elegance of the educated snob:

> They lead sheep to the rivulet with a drum
> Dancing with absolutely natural grace
> Remembered from the dark past whence we come.
> The whole thing was more like a bloody picnic.
> Bottles of white rum and a brawling booth.
> They tie the lamb up, then chop off the head,
> And ritualistic take turns drinking the blood.
> Great stuff, old boy; sacrifice, moments of truth.
> Poopa, da' was a fete! I mean it have
> Free rum free whisky and some fellars beating
> Pan from one of them band in Trinidad
> And everywhere you turn was people eating
> And drinking and don't name me but I think
> They catch his wife with two tests up the beach
> While he drunk quoting Shelley . . .
> (Black writer chap, one of them Oxbridge guys).[13]

It is significant that this peasant viewpoint uses the dialect rhythms exploited by the calypso. For they demonstrate that here

Walcott is manipulating those dialect rhythms which are the staple of the calypsonian's polymetric design, and which Edward Brathwaite feels have been under-exploited by the West Indian writer. And once again, the writer's interest in the form and themes of the calypso hinges on the ambiguities and paradoxes of calypsonian irony. In this instance, Walcott has imitated the calypsonian's characteristic use of dialect forms as a mask. The poem disguises trenchant satire with the dialect's playful rhythms ("Poopa — da was — a fete"), the racy delivery ("And drinking and don't name me but I think . . ."), and playful diction ("two tests"). Walcott's use of the dialect rhythms as an ironic mask is comparable with Sparrow's satiric disguises in songs like "Lulu," "Congo Man," and "Maria." And in the song, "Monica," Sparrow approximates the tradition of the blues by using this bouyant style to disguise the everyday tragedies and "near-tragedies" of peasant life:

>Then she say to me
>'Sparrow Ah think Ah makin' a baby
>But oh! Ah don't know
>Who the father or who to give it to.'
>She want to help she out
>But I planning to back out
>So I turn an' ask she
>What she husband goin' do 'bout that.
>>'Me no know me dear
>>Like the man he ain' care
>>The man he does leave me here alone
>>For weeks he don' come home
>>I have to depen'
>>On mah seaman frien'
>>When mah seaman frien'
>>Bring they frien'
>>Then ah have cash to spen'.'

The incongruity of the comic tone serves a dual purpose. It acts as Monica's defensive reflex against her own plight; and, simultaneously, it mimics the cold-blooded detachment of the narrator's determination to "back out" rather than to help.

This comic mask for tragedy has also found its way into the West Indian novel. Austin Clarke, as we have already seen, uses specific songs to dramatize his psycho-sexual themes in *Meeting Point*. And in this work he also follows the traditions of the calypso mask by disguising tragedy with the comic forms of dialect. Bernice Leach's account of Clotelle, another West Indian immigrant in Canada, is typical:

Clotelle buy-up silvers, knife and fork, spoon, sugar bowl, cream bowl, with Clotelle's initials and insignias carved in them. And the salesman-crook told Clotelle they weren't hard to pay for. But when the first instalment payment came, ninety-five dollars and five cents! Clotelle borrowed money from Sacrificial Finance Company and had to turn round and borrow money *needlessly* from Withold Corporation to pay back Sacrificial, and still the interest was mounting up, higher than the skies. And then, one fine day, Clotelle start looking for a new job, where nobody won't find her. But she didn't know that although this Toronto is a large city, it ain't so damn big that a finance company can't track you down, and find you, and pin you to the ground, Jesus Christ, till they squeeze every last drop of blood and payments outta you, till that debt squared-off. Three people was looking for Clotelle. They take out search warrant for her blood. 'Twas Sacrificial — Lord, deliver me ever from them clutches! — Withold and the silver people. And when they found Clotelle ... Bram! The finance-man and the bailiff-man or whoever the hell he was, plus the garnishee-man, all three o' them pounced on Clotelle, and when they get up offa Clotelle, the Hospital fired Clotelle, and she was *back in the same white woman kitchen,* working off her fat" (pp. 126-127).

The comic incongruities of the Clotelle "saga" are similar to those in Sparrow's "Monica." They are a defense mechanism with which Bernice protects herself from the grim implications of Clotelle's fate; and at the same time they imitate the heartlessness of the socio-economic machine which has Clotelle in its clutches. And this ironic juxtaposition of the satiric and the defensive is even more dramatic when this comic incongruity is applied to the tragedy of death itself, specifically, the death of Lottie, another West Indian immigrant. And the narrator of this tragedy, Dots uses a comically laconic style which is at once self-defensive and bitterly descriptive of the callous Canadian motorist whose car struck Lottie down in an accident: " 'Lottie dead,' Dots repeated, without too much emotion; as if she was reporting the death of a dog in the street . . . 'Appears like Lottie was going up Bloor Street, and she put out her hand to cross through one o' them blasted crosswalk-things, and . . . even though Lottie put out her hand to point, that man driving the motorcar came right on, and *bruggadungdung!* . . . dead." Bernice's angry reflections on the mishap continue in the vein of Dots' narrative: "All the money that poor girl saved up, all those five years working off her arse, and saving ninety-nine cents out of a dollar, turning her eyes 'gainst the luxuries o' this world, and setting them on necessary things, and now, out of the blue, bram! a blasted motor-car . . ." (pp. 15-16, 17).

Altogether then, a calypsonian such as Sparrow is a sophisticated artist whose work ("Lulu") demonstrates a critical self-awareness of the scope and functions of calypso as satire. Moreover, songs like "Congo Man," "Maria," and "Monica" ironically explore those racial and cultural experiences which shape the Afro-West Indian identity, and which provide the Caribbean writer with his primary themes. And, generally, the tensions and complexities of that cultural identity are reproduced by the ironic structure of the calypso. Both the calypsonian and his society mask a serious awareness of past suffering and present deprivation behind the old stereotype of the "happy" native in island paradises. On the whole, this ironic posture, together with his dialect forms and distinctively "ethnic" materials, establish the calypsonian's art as the direct expression of the Afro-West Indian experience. And it is this expressiveness which attracts the West Indian writer.

In view of this obvious attraction, it is not surprising that one writer, Samuel Selvon of Trinidad, has written about the composition of calypsoes. Indeed, Selvon's short-story, "Calypsonian," is a penetrating, fictional study of the cultural genesis of calypso. The story is not an anthropological or historical exercise: it does not pretend to investigate the calypso's genesis in an antiquarian sense. What Selvon does emphasize is the organic relationship between the society and the creation of a calypso song — between the artist's socia-economic environment, on the one hand, and on the other hand, both the calypsonian's themes and the actual *process* of composition. Accordingly, Selvon's calypsonian, Razor Blade, is one of Trinidad's hungry unemployed who survives as a beggar, thief, and calypso-writer. His personal deprivation reflects a broader social problem: "It had a time when things were really brown in Trinidad, and Razor Blade couldn't make a note nohow, no matter what he do, everywhere he turn, people telling him they ain't have work. It look like is work scarce like gold, and six months now he ain't working" (*Caribbean Literature,* p. 72).

Significantly, these are precisely the milieu and experience out of which Razor Blade's calypso emerges:

And he don't know why, but same time he get a sharp idea for a calypso. About how a man does catch royal when he can't get a work noway. The calypso would say about how he sees real hard days: he start to think up words right away as he walking in the rain:

> It had a time in this colony
> When everybody have money excepting me
> I can't get a work no matter how I try
> It looks as if good times pass me by (pp. 76-77).

Moreover, Selvon uses the occasion of the calypso's birth to emphasize the parallels between his own work and the calypsonian's art. For Razor Blade's themes, and the experiences which shape his calypso, are Selvon's subject. Like the calypso, the short-story is rooted in the life-style of Trinidad's poor and underprivileged. At the same time, the rhythmic patterns of Razor Blade's song disguise and counterbalance his theme of deprivation in the usual traditions of calypsonian irony. So does Selvon's short-story. The description of Razor Blade as a half-hearted, small-time thief is typical, for here Selvon juxtaposes Razor Blade's jaunty bearing and poverty, the bravado with which he determines to steal, and the cowardice which restrains him. And this personal mask which Razor Blade imposes on his own actions, and on his calypsoes, appears in Selvon's narrative style — Razor Blade's hardship and fright are described in playful language:

> Well, it don't take plenty to make a t'ief. All you have to do is have a fellar catching his royal, and can't get a work no way, and bam! By the time he make two three rounds he bounce something somewhere, an orange from a tray, or he snatch a bread in a parlor, or something.
> Like how he bounce the shoes.
> So though he frighten like hell and part of him going like a pliers, Razor Blade playing victor brave boy and whistling as he go down the road.
> The only thing now is that he hungry (p. 73).

In effect, Selvon's account of the birth of a calypso becomes self-descriptive. He illuminates the cultural roots and ironic forms which the literary artist shares with the calypsonian. And in illustrating organic links between the calypso and the West Indian's written literature, Selvon emphasizes the interchangeability of "literary" and calypsonian art. Brathwaite has reminded us that the calypsonian is an artist. Now Selvon, together with his fellow novelists and poets, have demonstrated that the West Indian writer is a calypsonian.

FOOTNOTES

1. Clarence Farmer, *Soul on Fire* (New York, 1969), p. 111.
2. *The Complete Poems of Paul Dunbar* (New York, 1911), p. 71.
3. Ralph Ellison, *Shadow and Act,* Signet ed. (New York, 1966), pp. 90, 91.
4. Edward Brathwaite, "Prelude," in *Rights of Passage* (London, 1967), p. 3.

5. George Lamming, *Pleasures of Exile* (New York, 1960), p. 90.
6. Paule Marshall, *Brown Girl Brownstones* (New York, 1959), p. 150.
7. Derek Walcott, "Travelogue," in *Caribbean Literature: An Anthology,* ed. G. R. Coulthard (London, 1966), p. 71.
8. Edward Brathwaite, "Gordon Rohlehr's 'Sparrow and the Language of the Calypso' " *Caribbean Quarterly,* XIV (March-June, 1968), p. 91.
9. Sparrow songs quoted in this paper are "Lulu," "Maria," and "Monica,' from *Sparrow.* Radio Corporation of America, LPB-9035; and "Congo Man," from *Mighty Sparrow: Trinidad Heat Wave,* Scepter Records, M10003.
10. Ismith Khan, *The Obeah Man* (London, 1964), p. 129.
11. See Frantz Fanon, *Black Skin White Masks,* trans. Charles Lam Markmann (New York, 1962), pp. 41-62, 141-209 (Originally published as *Peau Noire, Masques Blancs,* 1952); Calvin C. Hernton, *Sex and Racism in America,* Evergreen ed. (New York, 1966), *passim;* Eldridge Cleaver, *Soul on Ice,* Delta ed. (New York, 1968), pp. 155-204.
12. Austin C. Clarke, *The Meeting Point* (Toronto, 1967), pp. 71-72.
13. Derek Walcott, *Selected Poems* (New York, 1964), p. 11.

AN ASPECT OF AFRICAN AND CARIBBEAN THEATER IN FRENCH
by
HAROLD A. WATERS

This essay examines the characteristics and the present state of African and Caribbean French-language theatre. I hope that it is not catechistic to list the States of the world invited to the second congress "des Etats entièrement ou partiellement francophones" (Phillippe Decraene, in *Le Monde,* March 15-16, 1970), which was held in Niamey, Niger, from March 16 through 20, 1970: Canada, Haiti, Belgium, France, Luxembourg, Monaco, Switzerland, Lebanon, Tunisia, Algeria, Morocco, Mauritania, Senegal, Mali, Guinea, Upper Volta, Ivory Coast, Niger, Dahomey, Togo, Chad, Central African Republic, Cameroon, Gabon, Congo-Brazzaville, Congo-Kinshasa, Rwanda, Burundi, Mauritius, Malagasy Republic, Laos, Cambodia, Democratic Republic of Vietnam, South Vietnam. One can pick out the countries included under the rubric of African and Caribbean, and one can add to the list of French-speaking areas France's overseas départements (which are certainly not in the same departmental category as the Hauts-de-Seine!) : Guadeloupe, French Guyana, Martinique, and Réunion.

It is not my intention to treat all these political entities one after the other. Indeed, nowhere near half of them have produced French plays the news of which has crossed their borders. Simply, I want to discuss certain pertinent questions like: (1) What are the content of the indigenous product, especially inofar as such contents differ from those of Occidental plays? (2) what is the quantitative state of African and Caribbean French theater? (3) what is the role of French-language theater in the areas studied as opposed to the role in them of the other French-language arts? (4) what is the role of the French language in areas where it is in competition with indigenous tongues?

1. Contents

In 1956 Arthur Adamov defined Social Theater as that theater "qui mettrait en question la société même où nous vivons" (*Ici et maintenant* [Paris: Gallimard, 1964], p. 31). This succinct definition unquestionably applies to the whole theatrical output of the areas concerned, although not for a reason that Adamov could have had in mind, namely, that they are changing and certainly *must* change if they are ever to be other than the euphemism known as developing or emerging nations, not to speak of a sub-Saharan esthetic that places all aspects of life, political and social included, under the aegis of culture. Adamov directly emphasized the political band on the social science spectrum, but it is self-evident that for the colonial or excolonial lands society must change far more than just politically.

It should also be pointed out that Social Theater is distinguishable much more by its contents than by its form. In the following forms that Social Theater has taken in the West, the same *forms* could have urged beatification for Eva Peron. Straight and serious drama (for example: Michel Vinaver, *Les Coréens* [Paris: Gallimard, 1956]); heavy satire (Jean-Paul Sartre, *Nekrassov* [Paris: Gallimard, 1957]); review (Raymond Gerbal, *Paris-Chaud* [not published, but performed winter 1968-1969 at the Romain Rolland Villejuif); redoings of the classics (Patrice Chéreau's *Don Juan* [performed winter 1968-1969 at the Gérard Philippe in Sartrouville]); radical experimentalization (André Benedetto, *Zone rouge* [Paris-Honfleur: P. J. Oswald, 1969]); collective creations (Jean-Pierre Bisson and others, *Matin rouge* [performed spring 1969 at the Plaisance]). Even agitprop could have its anodine shipboard parallels!

So while African and Caribbean *Social Theater* (if the *point* be granted that all of it can be so described) has every right to contain the typically Occidental attacks against, say, Hungary, Vietnam, the fate of the Jews in Russia, the Marines in Nicaraugua, Czechoslovakia, Brazilian torture and Brazilian extermination of the Indians, and the like, what particularizes it is something else than worldwide "injustice." Here for example is what Michel Habart wrote in 1958, while the French flag still flew over Algeria:

> Freres, voici la fin de votre entracte. Le rideau va se lever.
> Les treteaux se veulent table rase en undecor de printemps.
> Votre histoire va se chanter sur d'autres notes que celles de

> vos complaintes d'agonie. Nous allons enfin baisser nos mains que nous serrions sur nos tympans pour ne plus vous entendre. Le visage de ce peuple, qu'ils ont voulu souiller, profaner, denaturer, jusqu'en ses racines les plus secretes, se profile a l'avant-scene de l'histoire. Auront-ils assez de pudeur, ou de remords, pour se taire, ecouter, et en rougir? (preface to Henri Krea, *Theatre algerien* [Honfleur-Tunis: P. J. Oswald, 1968], p. 12).

The colonial system simplified the problem of the subjugated, or, rather, made one problem more than all others: that of being freed from it. Implicit in Habart's prophetic clarion call was not only this problem but a second one, when the first had been resolved. Cut off from their roots by the imposition of foreign cultures, there would remain to the newly free the important tasks of discovering their past, expressing their present, and looking into the future. Here lies a sharp distinction between the possible content of excolonial theater and the theater of the rest of the world. Behind the singing of the past in an Occidental play there could well be a reactionary motive, whereas the same song in an excolonial play could be the answer to an urgent and legitimate social need.

Whether the theater as it is known in the West is primarily a Western form is a moot point, but to the extent that it is so the theater of the areas concerned must ironically use a colonial art form to express the past, the present, and the hopes of the future. In a preface to the published volume of Cheik Ndao's *L'Exil d'Albouri* (Honfleur-Paris: P. J. Oswald, 1967), Bakary Traoré summarized the main (sometimes questionable) stances of his important *Le Théâtre négro-africain et ses fonctions sociales* (Paris: Présence Africaine, 1958) which bear quoting here *in toto*. Rejecting the idea of an excolonial theater that would dwell exclusively on the often sanguinary exploits of legendary African rulers, he stated:

> Le theatre africain sera epique ou ne sera pas. Il y a longtemps que Cheik Ndao a compris cette exigence fondamentale.
>
> Quels doivent etre les caracteres de ce theatre? Il y a d'abord un espect intellectuel: faire reconnaitre les civilisations africaines, par une prise de conscience de la singularite de nos problemes.
>
> Deuxieme aspect: l'aspect moral, ethique. Par une demarche intellectuelle, rester fidele a nos valeurs . . . .
>
> Enfin le theatre africain doit avoir un troisieme aspect: l'aspect prospectif. Depassant le lyrisme, moment de la prise de conscience, nous devons atteindre le realisme qui n'est pas description du reel mais un essai de participation totale a la

realite d'un peuple, passant par une participation commune. Et c'est peut-etre dans le *realisme epique* que sera la reponse du theatre negro-africain — tout comme la tragedie de *Sophocle* etait la reponse du peuple grec a l'Histoire, cette tragedie, reponse collective aux "pressions historiques" qui ont fait du peuple grec ce qu'il fut dans une large mesure: "le defenseur de la democratie et de la liberte" (p. 10).

This order is perhaps too tall, too restrictive: In the Father's house there are many mansions. Theater so described would be *distinctively* Negro-Africain — North African and Caribbean theater would follow suit in a parallel way — but the excolonial problem is too complex for excolonial dramatists to be so limited in their choice of content. Thus Traoré's prescriptions cannot be the only ones. Still, the epic route is the one taken by many African writers. The rising peoples clearly need to find their identity, as individuals and as groups. These groups can be of many sorts — for example, ethnic or political. In *La Mort du Damel* (published with *Les Derniers Jours de Lat Dior* [Paris: Présence Africaine, 1965]) Senegal's governmental figure Amadou Cissé Dia goes against Traoré's counsel by giving to his country, for legend's sake, the bloody story of the Damel Teigne Macadou Fall. In *El Hadj Omar* (Honfleur-Paris: P. J. Oswald, 1968) the Haitian Gérard Chenet recounts the title-character's thwarted efforts to unify black Africa under the crescent of Islam in the nineteenth century. And of course Traoré's prophesy eventually may well be realized in part, through excolonial plays which preach, as only their authors may be able to do, a pan-nationalism encompassing not a continent but the entire world.

Meanwhile the necessity remains of identifying the past and identifying or understanding the present, with the desire always in mind of suggesting union of any sort that is feasible. The acuteness of this need is perhaps nowhere better demonstrated than by a confrontation of certain passages from three plays, *Et les chiens se taisent* (Paris: Présence Africaine, 1963) by Aimé Césaire, *Des Voix dans une prison* (published in volume form under the title *Chants pour hâter la most du temps des Orphée* along with that play and with *La Voix des sirénes* and *Orphée nègre* [Honfleur-Paris: P. J. Oswald, 1967]) by Daniel Boukman, and *Eïa! Manmaille là!* (Honfleur-Paris ; P. J. Oswald, 1968) by Auguste Macouba. All three are from Martinique. In *Et les chiens se taisent* the story of the life, revolutionary acts, and execution of the anonymous Rebel of an anonymous Caribbean island, here the Rebel sings of all the islands on the chain:

> Iles heureuses;
> jardins de la reine
> je me laisse deriver dans la nuit d'epices de tornades et de saintes images
> et le varech agrippe de ses petits doigts d'enfants mon barissement futur d'epave ... (p. 94).

Later the Chorus intones:

> je me souviens du matin des iles
> le matin petrissant de l'amande et du verre
> les grives riaient dans l'arbre a graines
> et le veson ne sentait pas mauvais
> non
> dans le matin fruite! (p. 110).

The play concludes:

> LA RECITANTE. — Je suis une de vous, Iles! *(Le Recitant et la Recitante vacillent sur leurs jambes puis s'effondrent, le choeur sort a reculons.) (Vision de la Caraibe bleue semee d'iles d'or et d'argent dans la scintillation de l'aube.)* (pp. 121-122).

Toward the end of *Des Voix dans une prison* the Future personified names these same islands one by one in her speech to *this* play's condemned revolutionary; she finishes by:

> archipel a la verte chevelure de canne deployee dans le vent
> BEL ARC
> que bandera demain
> LE PEUPLE LIBRE DES AMERIQUES DEYANQUINISEES
> Caravane de douleurs
> mais surtout d'esperances
> COURAGE mes iles COURAGE! (p. 124).

Macouba's *Eïa! Man-maille là!* describes the popular uprising of December 1959 at Fort-de-France, Martinique. At the beginning of the action an offstage Echo says: "Imaginez-vous, cette guirlande de terres, ce chapelet de miettes; pays d'hibiscus et de soleil. Ici, multicéphales se sont rassemblés: le Noir, le Blanc, le Rouge et le Jaune. Voici les ANTILLES!" (p. 22). Directly following, the Echo enumerates the islands just as had the Future in Boukman's play! The similarities are no coincidence, nor, probably, did the playwrights know each other's works when each wrote his own. One after the other was simply dramatizing the overwhelming need for immediate or eventual unity in their common area of origin.

The distinction between two key terms should be noted. *Ex*colonialism is pure and simple the situation of a region that has been freed from colonialism. *Neo*colonialism is the situation that prevails in an excolonial country which finds itself, under its own leaders, to be in effect dominated by the same sort of Brechtian gangsters it had known before. If Haiti and the Dominican Republic saw their last colonial woes over with in, respectively, 1844 and 1865, these two Caribbean nations are and for a long time have been victims of the enemy from within. Neocolonialism thus can wreak something very akin to the situation against which the social dramatists of the West are so inalterably opposed. One is thus returned full circle: An appeal for unity, for respect of traditional values, if made under the aegis of neocolonialism, would no longer be a true social appeal and would be as suspect as if it emanated from a General Franco.

By way of examples, in 1969 Haiti made being a Communist a capital offense; August Macouba is in fact an alias. Daniel Boukman, a French Army deserter, lives in Algeria. In his 1962 *Les Malheurs de Tchakô* (Honfleur-Paris: P. J. Oswald, 1968) the Ivory Coaster Charles Nokan had a peasant say: "Nous produisons pour les princes et fonctionnaires qui vivent en une insolente opulence" (p. 33), and his title-character's final words are: "Je ne désire pas mourir maintenant. Après le désert obscur, je veux la vie dure du combattant, et les fleures bleues de l'existence" (pp. 95-96). In 1964 Nokan was arrested by the authorities of his country for the subversive content of his writings. Freed from prison in 1965, he now lives in Paris. Generally and theatrically, present distinctive and "excusable" nationalism or pan-nationalism of the new countries must be kept under suspicious and close observation, because either theme can be utilized by the forces of reaction!

2. Quantity

A glance at only the Présence Africaine catalog indicates how well black and *Arab* French-language literature is faring, not to speak of the catalogs of Fernand Nathan, Le Seuil, François Maspero, P. J. Oswald. It will be recalled too that Mali novelist Yambo Oulogaem won the 1968 Renaudot Prize for *Le Devoir de violence* (Paris, Le Seuil). In his recent letter-article for *Le Monde des Livres* (August 2, 1969) Robert Cornevin wrote:

> . . . ce qu'il faut noter, c'est l'extraordinaire floraison litteraire de l'Afrique noire d'expression francaise, les centaines d'ecrivains africains departis de Dakar a Brazzaville, d'Abidjan a Yaounde, de Libreville a Cotonou et Bamako, de Conakry a Niamey, de Bangui a Bujumbura, qui contribuent a accroitre le patrimoine francophone dont la richesse justifierait, a present, des etudes particulieres sur les litteratures nationales.

In Africa, one Normal School, two national theater companies, and one important festival played or are playing primordial roles in the subject at hand, both quantitatively and qualitatively: l'Éole William Ponty in Senegal, the Théâtre Daniel Sorano in Dakar under the direction of Maurice Sonar Senghor, the Centre Culturel de Hammamet in Tunisia under Tahar Guiga, the first and grandiose Pan-African Cultural Festival in Algiers, held in the summer of 1969.

In 1933 l'École William Ponty was situated in Sébikotane, in what was then part of French West Africa and what is now Senegal. Beginning that year, the students, who came from all over French West Africa and French Equatorial Africa, were given the vacation project of recording some sociological aspects of their home communities. They could do this in dramatic form, and those who elected this option had to write their plays in French. In 1937 a William Ponty troupe reached Paris and was much acclaimed. Theatrical activity at this school flourished far into the 1940's, and also served to inspire similar projects throughout French colonial Africa. It is exact to see in the William Ponty "summer homework" the essential birth of black African French-language theater.

When the Daniel Sorano's own two directors, Maurice Sonar Senghor and Raymond Hermantier, are not in action it imports other "enlightened" ones like Jean-Marie Serreau, that eminent proponent of African theater. The Sengalese (cultured) public thus has brought before it plays performed in French which were either written originally in that language by Frenchmen, black Africans, North Africans, Caribbeans, or which have been translated into French from the other world tongues. 1969 examples of this last category are *Monsieur Pot de Vin et consort,* an adaptation of Gogol's *The Inspector General,* which was directed by Senghor, and a *Macbeth* directed by Hermantier. To provide a single instance of the activities of the Tunisian Centre Culturel, Aimé Césaire's (not *La* but) *Une Tempête* (Paris: Le Seuil, 1969) premiered in the same summer at the Festival International de Hammamet, under the direction of the much-traveled Serreau.

The Pan-African Cultural Festival in Algiers was successful from many points of view, notably that of the theater contest. I would not wish to repeat very much of what has been said by others, perhaps best of all by Bakary Traoré, the author of the already-cited *Le Théâtre négro-africain et ses fonctions sociales,* in "Le Théâtre africain au Festival Culturel Panafricain d'Alger"

(*Présence Africaine,* no. 72 [4ᵉ trim. 1969], pp. 179-189). Briefly, plays could be submitted in either of Africa's *linguae francae,* English and French, or in one of the indigenous tongues. Of the twelve plays presented, one was in English, one in Arabic, one in Ghanian, one in Yoruba, and *eight in French.* The gold medal was bestowed on the Senegalese offering by Cheik Ndao, *L'Exil d'Albouri* (Honfleur-Paris: P. J. Oswald, 1967).

3. French-language Theater and the Other French-language Arts

In the woreword to his long study for *Le Monde des Livres* (June 21, 1969) entitled "L'Afrique noire d'expression française" Jacques Chevrier warned:

> Nous avons laisse deliberement dans l'ombre la poesie et le theatre, celebres a plus d'un titre, comme en temoignent les seuls noms de Leopold Senghor, Aime Cesaire et Jean-Joseph Rabearivelo. A une periode lyrique coincident avec un monde inacceptable, et ou seule la poesie etait porteuse d'espoir (on songe naturellement aux negro spirituels des Noirs d'Amerique), a succede pour les ecrivans africains l'age de la prose.

Comparatively, another glance at the Présence Africaine catalog would not support Chevrier's view in regard to either theater or poetry. Also, reference to the subject-matter of just the plays this essay happens to mention will indicate that, even with the question of lyricism aside (why cannot there be a practical flavor to lyricism!), Negro-African dramatists are indeed involved in the same "prosaic" world as the novelists and the short-story writers, with whom Chevrier's study deals exclusively. And in considering the audience one may in fact wonder if the theater, as opposed to prose written to be read, is not a genre more accessible — surely in potential and quite likely in the actual case — to the peoples of developing nations.

4. French as a Rival of Indigenous Tongues

What is the role of French in the former French colonies of Africa — a similar question applies to the anglophone areas — as opposed to that of the native tongues? The problem suggested here is a major one because, reverting to the idea of the newer nations, much of their populace speaks only the native ones; indeed, one may ask, why should it be expected to master other tongues? Most aspiring writers of non-European stock on the African continent probably know either English or French, perhaps both. For example, the Nigerian dramatist Ola Balogun (*Shango-Le Roi éléphant* [Honfleur: Oswald, 1968]) writes with ease in either.

While they no doubt know one or more African languages as well, one can think of many reasons — the main one is to communicate with as many people as possible — for the large majority of them to prefer English or French as their main mode of expression. It should be added that these generalities overlook the few examples of African writers who are not of European stock, nor are blacks or Arabs, for example, the writers of Indonesian-Polynesian or Indian descent in the Malagasy Republic.

One must certainly lay low the idea that the francophone world includes all the inhabitants of areas that one did belong or still do to France. A typical expression of this idea was made by Sanche de Grammont, in his *The French — portrait of a people* (New York: G. P. Putnam's Sons, 1969) :

> Instead of the babble of tongues predicted by the Old Testament, the number of languages is shrinking, and nearly half the world population speaks in a borrowed idiom, whether in Washington, Buenos Aires, Rio de Janeiro, or Dakar. The most tenacious form of colonialism is linguistic: 8,000,000 Belgians, 10,000,000 Canadians, 6,000,000 Pacific islanders, and 55,000,000 Africans speak, or try to speak, the language of Descartes (p. 259).

Such naïveté can be shared by Africans as well. In an article for *Le Monde* (December 3, 1969), J. Champion reported that the President of the Congo-Kinshasa, General Joseph-Désiré Mobutu, has often claimed that his country represents, "avec ses quatorze à quinze millions de Congolais, le second pays francophone du monde . . ." Champion went on to say:

> Tous les gens avertis savent en effet que le francais n'est parle et ecrit correctement au Congo-Kinshasa que par une infime minorite, 1 a 2% de la population totale. Que dire du "petit" Senegal dont les lient economiques et culturels avec la France sont si etroits, et dont le role du president est si eminent dans la francophonie, alors que la majorite des adultes ne comprend pas le francais et n'a meme aucune possibilite de l'apprendre, comme le faisait remarquer Albert Doppagne a la Biennale de la langue francaise a Quebec en septembre 1967? Et il ajoutait que "la qualite actuelle du francais pratique par les representants de la grande francophonie (ceux qui ont adopte le francais comme langue officielle) va de zero jusqu'a l'erudition d'un membre de la commission du dictionnaire de l'Academie francaise;" ce qui s'applique a toute l'Afrique francophone, mais particulierement bien au Senegal.

Those parts of the world that have undergone a French "experience" probably will keep French as a *lingua franca* long into the future. It is to be noted though that the so-called francophone political entities in the areas studied do not look on French with an equal amount of appreciation. The French of France enjoys considerable prestige by the rich of Haiti, for example, although Creole is the language all Haitians speak. In the African countries with which this study is concerned, France is either *the* official language, *an* official language, a tolerated language, or one that persists *come malgré tout*.

Expediency of one sort or another is the simple reason for the survival of the French language, where it vies with "native" tongues. How else, presently and in the *near* future, are Algerians and Senegalese to communicate? For the very same reason, theater and the other language arts in the present and former French domains are bound to depend lingeringly upon French. A francophone African playwright, contrariwise to his ethnic "duties," will, to repeat, want to influence a maximum audience; thus, either side of this question can be construed to be the side of the angels, and it is a foregone conclusion as to which side most such playwrights will turn.

But this is truer of the subSahara than of North Africa. While the former area is divided by or into countless tongues, so many of them unrelated, it is quite possible that classical Arabic will eventually unify linguistically North Africa and the whole Arab world. When this might come to be it not perfectly clear, as is demonstrable in the case of Algeria alone, where linguistic difficulties occur, even aside from the question of French there. Not only is classical Arabic "pitted against" the country's various Arabic dialects (among which often one can just barely make oneself understood), but there are also non-semitic tongues, like those spoken by the Berbers. While French is still used in the country's secondary and higher education, there is an attempt to play it down progressively, and one may assume that some day — a day sooner than in many other presently francophone countries — Algeria will not be the froncophone bloc by any whit of the imagination. Still, in the fall of 1970 arabization met a setback when except for the lowest years of education it was decreed that French was to be the language of the classroom! The linguistic situation referred to is well illustrated if one thinks of the many definitions that would come to mind if one heard the term "a captured Algerian"! And while (classical) arabization in Algeria continues apace, or tries to, *El Moudjahid,* Algiers' daily newspaper, runs 87,000 copies of its French edition and only 3,000 of its edition in classical Arabic!

Except to a small degree in West Africa for Wolof and to a greater degree in East Africa for Swahili, the Sub-Sahara enjoys no possibility of a non-French or non-English linguistic carrot like classical Arabic. It wil lhave to depend politically on French and/or English, and the language arts will naturally follow along. Still, North Africa's shorter-range advantage may well disappear in the far future, if it then seems that classical Arabic is simply not enough for satisfactory co-existence in the world community. While the linguistic map of that far future depends too much on conjecture at this point to warrant considerable examination here and now, here are two linguistic predictions, one short-range, one long-range.

The short-range one is that African and Caribbean theater will continue to be written predominantly in the languages of the former or present occupiers; absolutely so in the Caribbean, where the indigenous or slave tongues have now been killed out, relatively so in the sub-Sahara, whose political entities have communication problems within themselves, among themselves, and in the world as a whole; less so in North Africa, where classical Arabic waits in the wings. Here though let me skirt the problem of Creole, which could (if not should) some day take over from Dutch, English, French, and Spanish as *the* official language of much of the Caribbean.

The long-range prediction deals a *coup de grâce* to the French language in general. Even in France, many scientists have to speak English among themselves when they are discussing their particular science. This tendency grows in the sciences, in diplomacy, and will it not be the case, if it is not already beginning to be so, in the language arts as well? One can imagine resistance to the trend in the Russian and Chinese blocs of today, but may there well not be a gradual reversal as the distant future comes near?

In any case, indigenous peoples who do not comprehend tongues other than their own have a right to expect public subsidization of translations into their idioms of certain products of the world's language arts. This is not the occasion to set up a priority table on such a count, but by way of an example close to home a Wolof-speaking, non-French-speaking Senegalese should have a real social right to a performance in Wolof of Cheik Ndao's *L'Exil d'Albouri*. There is a taint of neocolonialism or mandarinism in not granting him this right. What a supreme though probably necessary irony that a social dramatist may often not write his plays in the language of his own people!

THE NEGRO THEATER IN BRAZIL*
by
ABDIAS DO NASCIMENTO

Several questions were raised in my mind by the tragedy of that unfortunate Negro whom the genius of Eugene O'Neill had transformed into *The Emperor Jones*. The production I attended took place in the Municipal Theater in Lima, Peru, and the impact of the play itself was enhanced by another startling fact: The role of the hero was played by a white actor in blackface. In those days of 1941, I knew little about the theater, since my profession is economics — in fact, just before going to see the play, I had given a lecture at the Seminar on Economics of the University of San Marcos — and I did not have the technical knowledge to assess the interpretive abilities of Hugo Devieri, the actor. But something told me that he lacked the emotional strength required by the role and that it could be brought out on stage only by an actor of the Negro race. Why a white man made up as a Negro? I asked myself. For lack of a Negro actor? I remembered, however, that in my own country, where at that time there were 20 million Negroes out of a total population of 60 million, I had never seen a play in which the leading role had been played by an actor of my race. Could it be, therefore, that Brazil was not a real racial democracy? My ruminations went further: In my country, so proud of having resolved the problem of blacks and whites living side by side in an exemplary way, the presence of Negroes on stage should have been quite normal, not only in minor and comic roles, as was the case, but in any role whatsoever — Hamlet or Antigone — as long as the actors had the requisite talents. What happened was actually quite the opposite: Even the part of Emperor Jones, if produced

*Originally appeared in *African Forum*, reprinted here with the kind permission of the author.

in Brazil, would of necessity have been played by a white actor in blackface, following the age-old example of productions of *Othello*. Even in Brazilian plays — like *O Demonio Familiar* (The Family Demon), 1957, by Jose de Alencar or *Iaia Boneca*, 1938, by Ernani Fornari — the roles that could be played by Negro actors normally excluded the authentic Negro in favor of the caricature Negro.

This sad fact (or confirmation) called for a resolution on my part. It could be none other than the decision to do something to eradicate not only the absurdity of the situation as far as Negroes were concerned but also the cultural prejudices that were damaging my country. At the end of the play, I had reached a decision: On my return to Brazil, I would organize a theatrical group that would open the role of protagonist to the Negro, enable him to rise from his status as a secondary or folkloric character to become the *subject* and hero of the plays in which he appeared. Rather than as vindication or protest, I looked upon such a change as a defense of the cultural reality of Brazil and as a contribution to the humanism that respects all men and their diverse cultures.

Before 1944, when I made a reality of the Teatro Experimental do Negro (Experimental Theater of the Negro), known as the TEN, in Rio de Janeiro, other thoughts developed, as a result of which the original project became much more profound and complex. I asked myself: What could there be, besides the ornamental color bar, that justified the absence of the Negro on the Brazilian stage? Could the theory of their inability to play serious roles, their lack of artistic responsibility, be true? Was it that they were considered capable of playing only the picturesque "black-boy" or other folkloric characters? Could there be deeper implications, a basic difference of artistic conception or theatrical expression — perhaps a white aesthetic and a black aesthetic, produced by the conditioning of segregation and conflicting interests? There must have been something underlying that objective abnormality that existed back in the year 1944. Because to speak of genuine theater — the fruit of man's imagination and creative power — is to speak of plunging into the roots of life. And Brazilian life had excluded the Negro from its vital center only out of blindness or the deformation of reality. Thus we must go back in history to decipher the contradictions that face us and perhaps to find the illumination for the path that the Negro theater in Brazil must follow.

At the outset, we must repeat the obvious: A colony, Brazil was modeled upon the original mother country, Portugal. The Brazil of 1500 was simply the object of Portugal's predatory greed, a mere appendage of the Portuguese empire, an agricultural trading post; and the colonizers, rather than populating the land, devoted themselves to plundering the newly-discovered territory of all the gold and emeralds they could get to supply European markets. Since its axis was outside the country, the economic interest of the colonizers worked like a magnetic needle that pointed toward Europe via Portugal; and from Europe came everything, from manufactured goods to aesthetic models, from ideas and beliefs to social customs and manners, political and juridical institutions. When the incapacity of the natives for forced labor became evident in the first few years after the discovery, African slavery was introduced into the New World too by Portugal, the first of the European nations to become a slaver. It was not in vain that the Portuguese were the first Europeans to set foot on Sub-Sahara Africa.

Transplanted to America from Europe, the colonist brought with him Portuguese interests and all the mental baggage of his formation in the mother country. But what kind of formation was it for the African? Custom and a supposed anthropological knowledge had made a dogma out of the idea of the inferiority of the black race. The spurious ambitions of that imperialist rationalization were not limited to the political or economic spheres, however; they overflowed into the fields of ethics, aesthetics, and religion. The domination by force of the African was followed by his enforced migration, with the subsequent violence to his customs, traditions, and family organization. A truly cosmic vision of *whiteness* pressured and degraded the values of black metaphysics, black morals, black beauty. Katherine Dunham is right when she singles out as the most sensitive form of deprivation and usurpation the one that brings on spiritual inanition as the result of a cutting off of the roots of origin and tradition.

The anthropology and sociology practiced until recently in Brazil bore the unmistakeable traces of their overseas origins. In the exhaustive bibliography about the Negro, one discovers a strange Negro, far removed from those found on the streets, working in the factories, harvesting or planting coffee and sugar cane, living in the *favelas,* singing on the radio, shining shoes, trying to get into high school, and dreaming of a university degree. The social scientists, the authors of the books, were generally not people of evil intentions; most of them had generous feelings, and some had genuine friendship for the Negro. They were, however, conditioned by the anthropological outlook in the mother country, working under criteria that were inadequate for the context they proposed to analyze. Mistaken, they confused scientific prejudice with reality. Consequently, they turned the Negro into a *question, ethnographic material*; that is, the Negro-as-museum-piece, stuffed and transformed. His exotic (*ex-optic*) configuration aroused lively curiosity in the picturesqueness of his cooking, his love-making, the shape of his skull, his way of dancing and drumming as he worshipped his gods.

The African was the victim of double rape, spiritual and sexual; and the violation of his cultural origins corresponded to the violation of black women, who suffered even greater degradation than prostitution by being transformed into articles of use for the white colonists. For this reason, the assertion that tries to mask the malicious sexual domination of the Portuguese with a lack of racial intolerance is not valid. In fact, this despoilment — sexual despoilment — exposed the so-called natural tendency of the Portuguese toward miscegenation and even a certain Luso-tropicalism as a trick to bring on domestication. Despoiled in every definition of the word — even of their very humanity — the slaves became little more than tools, things, private property, which the Portuguese master made use of as he saw fit.

Thanks to the Negro's work and capacity for adaptation, he came to be the basic element in the formation of the Brazilian economy and in the ethnic and social make-up of the colony. It was the African who made possible the economic development of Brazil, just as slaves in the United States made possible the growth of its capitalist economy.

Although he had no classification in Brazil, living within a social structure that was developing around him as if he did not exist, the African slave nevertheless reacted. In every possible way he pursued the recapture of his freedom and dignity, setting up his *quilombos,* or refuges, for runaway slaves and trying to keep his customs alive.

One of the claims of imperialism was the propagation of the faith and the conversion of pagans. With the aim of saving the souls of the Indians and, conversely, of helping to maintain African slavery, the Jesuit missionaries came to Brazil. It was one of them — Father Jose de Anchieta— who made the first attempts at a theater in Brazil, for Anchieta wrote many religious plays in the European tradition, called *auto sacramental,* which were put on by Portuguese and converted Indians. The first of these was presented some time between 1567 and 1570 and bore the name *Auto da Pregacao Universal* (Play of Universal Preaching).

During the period of the Jesuit religious plays of the sixteenth century, the slaves too, during the season between Christmas and Epiphany, would present their own plays: the *Congada* or *Congo,* the *Quicumbre,* the *Quilombos* — of African origin — and the *Bumba-meu-boi,* whose origins are vague but which shows obvious adaptations by slaves with the inclusion of characters such as Mateus and Bastiao, "pet Negroes," the germ of the picturesque little Negro boys of the future. The latter, accepted during slavery, have come down to our times as the only Negro "actors" tolerated on the Brazilian stage. Slave skits and sketches were presented as if they were Portuguese *autos* of the sixteenth century or French medieval plays.

An unwritten theater in the African tradition of the Griots appeared — oral, anonymous, folkloric; even today the vitality of these collective manifestations can be seen in many sections of the country. The names of some of their actors have been preserved, and those of the slaves Caetano Lopes dos Santos and Maria Joaquina have been recorded — "King" and "Queen" of the *Congada* presented with great success in Rio de Janeiro in 1811. Another who was remembered was the former slave and actor Vitoriano for his interpretation in 1790 of *Tamerlao na Persia* (Tamerlaine in Persia) in Cuiaba in Mato Grosso.

As the colony developed demographically and its society became formed, the absence of white women became more serious and the sexual use of Negro women by the colonists became, in a manner of speaking, an institutionalized norm. A new ethnic and social class appeared, that of the mulatto. His status was ambivalent: The child of a slave woman was a slave; however, the bastard child of the master enjoyed certain concessions and privileges. The mulatto personified both the attraction and the repulsion that existed between the big house and the slave quarters. As a marginal figure, the mulatto was destined to fulfill certain functions of trust for the Portuguese such as overseer and slave-hunter, unpleasant and distasteful tasks. Later he was given another assignment — that of actor. It must be kept in mind that at that time the profession of actor was considered a base activity, "the most shameful of all . . . lower than the most infamous and criminal." Why, then, not open it to those restless mulattoes, as long as they covered their faces with "a coat of red and white paint"?

They not only acted on the stage but also took on other responsibilities, like the "mulatto and hunchbacked" Father Ventura, who built the Rio de Janeiro opera house in 1767. Between 1753 and

1771, in the suburb of Palha in Diamantina (Minas Gerais), a famous Negro woman, Chica da Silva, operated a private theater where the classical repertory of the period was presented. On the musical side — as composer as well as performer — the Negro contributed a great deal, as the important figure of the classical composer Father Jose Mauricio (1767-1830), music master of the Imperial Chapel, made clear.

By and large, the plays presented on the Brazilian stage were either by foreign authors or by Brazilians who followed European models in their works, in theme and in form. Thus, our historical formation was based on mimetic and repetitive action that reduced the dependent communities to simple reflexes of the mother country.

A Negro theater in Brazil would by necessity have to begin from a knowledge of the historical reality which would condition its revolutionary mission. With this in mind, the Teatro Experimental do Negro (TEN) took as its fundamental aim the task of redeeming in Brazil the values of Afro-Brazilian culture, so much denied and degraded by the pressure of white European culture; what was proposed was the social elevation of the Negro by means of education, culture, and art. We would have to work urgently on two fronts; to promote the denunciation of the mistakes and alienation purveyed by the studies of the Afro-Brazilian and to see that the Negro became aware of the objective situation in which he found himself. It was basic to the task that we not forget the spiritual slavery in which the Negro was kept before, as well as after, May 13, 1888, when he was theoretically freed from slavery. Theoretically, because the very same economic and social structure was maintained, and the freed Negro reaped no economic, social, or cultural dividend. The first task of TEN was to make literate its first participants — recruited from among workers, maids, slumdwellers without any definite occupation, humble civil servants — and to offer them a new attitude, a criterion of their own worth which would also make them see and perceive the position they occupied as Afro-Brazilians in the national context.

We began with the practical phase as distinguished from the academic and descriptive one. TEN was not interested in enlarging the number of monographs and other writings or in working out theories, but in a qualitative transformation in the social interaction between black and white. We could see that no other situation had ever needed more than ours the *removal* of Bertolt Brecht. A fabric woven by tradition was rising up between the observer and reality, deforming it. It was urgent to destroy it.

The first actors of TEN were ready. The next step was to find a play consonant with the artistic and social levels of the movement. What repertory existed was terribly weak — a few inferior plays in which the Negro appeared as the comic element, a picturesque character, or background material: *Demonio Familiar* (Family Demon), 1857, and *Mae* (Mother), 1859, both by Jose de Elencar; *Os Cancros Sociais* (Social Cancers), 1865, by Maria Ribeiro, *O Escravo Fiel* (The Faithful Slave), 1858, by Carlos Antonio Cordeiro; *O Escravocrata* (The Slave Owner), 1884, and *O Dote* (The Dowry), 1907, by Artur Azevedo, the first one with the collaboration of Urbano Duarte; *Calibar*, 1858, by Agrario de Meneses; the comedies of Martins Pena (1815-1848). And that was all there was. Not even one single script that reflected the dramatic situation of our existence. As Roger Bastide would say later, TEN was not a catharsis that could be expressed or brought on through laughter, since *the problem is infinitely more tragic; the squelching of black culture by white culture*. With no other possibilities, *The Emperor Jones* was a natural solution. It was a question of a meaningful play, one crossing the frontier of reality, of the rationalist logic of white culture. Did not the tragedy of that burlesque "Emperor" express a high moment of the magical conception of the world, the transcendental vision and the cosmic mystery of the everlasting marriage of the African with the pristine forces of nature? Man's mythical behavior was present in it. On the day-to-day level, however, Jones summed up the experience of the black man in the white world, where after having enslaved him, they freed him and cast him into the lowest levels of society. Led astray into a world that is not his, Brutus Jones learns the malicious value of money, lets himself be seduced by the mirage of power. On a Caribbean island he makes use of everything he has learned from the white man: By fraud he becomes "emperor"; he tricks, robs; hunted, he flees and comes face to face with his ultimate perdition.

We wrote a begging letter to Eugene O'Neill. No answer was ever so anxiously awaited. Who has never felt the solitude and pessimism that surrounds an opening gesture, when all there is to sustain it is the worth of a dream? From his sick-bed in San Francisco, on December 6, 1944, O'Neill answered us:

> You have my permission to produce *The Emperor Jones* without any payment to me, and I want to wish you all the success you hope for with your Teatro Experimental do Negro. I know very

well the conditions you describe in the Brazilian theatre. We had exactly the same conditions in our theatre before *The Emperor Jones* was produced in New York in 1920 — parts of any consequence were always played by blacked-up white actors. (This, of course, did not apply to musical comedy or vaudeville where a few Negroes managed to achieve great success.) After *The Emperor Jones,* played originally by Charles Gilpin and later by Paul Robeson, made a great success, the way was open for the Negro to play serious drama in our theatre. What hampers most now is the lack of plays, but I think before long there will be Negro dramatists of real merit to overcome this lack.

This generous cooperation and wise counsel had a decisive importance in our project, changing the mood of complete lack of support of the early days into confidence and euphoria. It helped us become able to conquer with intuition and heroism the inevitable expenses of sets, costumes, stagehands, electricians, callboys. We found in the actor Aguinaldo de Oliveira Camargo the strength capable of portraying the psychological complexity of Brutus Jones in an excellent translation by Ricardo Werneck de Aguiar. The most beautiful and least cumbersome sets that we could ever have hoped for were made by painter Enrico Bianco and have become classic in the Brazilian theater. With intense expectation, on May 8, 1945, in the Teatro Municipal of Rio de Janeiro, where never before had any Negro set foot either as actor or audience, TEN presented its opening production.

Critics were unanimous in their enthusiasm. Henrique Pongetti, dramatist and columnist of the influential *O Globo* said:

> He [Aguinaldo de Oliveira Camargo] is not a professional, he does not have a good idea of theatrical tempo, but he is a great actor in the sense that he can draw out of the audience the desired feelings by the strength of his primitive instinct for humanizing a role. . . . Brazilian Negroes (and whites too) now have a great dramatic actor: Aguinaldo de Oliveira Camargo. An anti-academic, rustic, instinctively great actor.

The atmosphere of pessimism and disbelief that preceded the premiere of TEN was expressed by the words of the writer Ascendino Leite:

> Our surprise was all the greater because of the doubts we had had relative to the choice of the repertory which started no less than with the inclusion of an author of the strength of expression that was O'Neill. We predicted that the Experimental Theater of the Negro would be a resounding failure. And we had privately already thought about the criticisms we would make about the audacity of this group of actors, almost all unknowns, who

dared to come before a public that was already beginning to see in the theater more than entertainment and rather a more direct form of penetrating the heart and of life and human nature. Aguinaldo Camargo in *The Emperor Jones* was therefore a revelation.

R. Magalhaes Junior, a member of the Brazilian Academy of Letters and a playwright, offered us his help:

The opening of the Theater of the Negro merits repetition because it was a notable presentation. Notable for several reasons. By its assured and firm direction. By the splendid and artistic sets by Enrico Bianco. And by the masterful interpretation by Aguinaldo de Oliveira Camargo of the role of Jones.

TEN had won its first victory. The Negro actor's clownish phase on the Brazilian stage was over. Grande Otelo, without doubt the finest actor that Brazil has, black or white, would still be able to exhibit his comic ability; but now it was known that other paths were open, and only the blindness or ill-will of producers would prevent the public from knowing, far beyond his well-known comedy, what the talent of Grande Otelo was capable of.

The first victory opened the way for the second phase: the creation of Brazilian plays for the Negro actor; but this was not to occur just yet. We did not intend to limit ourselves to the closed circle of a theater "for blacks only." But that would of necessity have to come first because of the existing circumstances. O'Neill's advice was absolutely correct. What the white man shows as the feelings of the Negro is one thing. His interior drama (that is to say, the Negro from within) is quite a different thing. The experience of being black in a white world is something that cannot be transferred. And in the sense in which we are speaking, calling Brazil a mixed nation is not valid. We know which models, values, and paragons of culture dominate, identify, and personalize Brazilian society. The definitive eradication of the anti-Negro peculiarity that permeated the community in its inner self and in its exterior expression had still not been brought about. Even today we are a two-faced nation: Abroad, Brazil is celebrated as a model of racial democracy; at home, there is still an attitude of mistrust toward the Negro as he insists upon the maintenance of the permanent values of his culture and origins. There are, however, sincere friends among Brazilian whites who respect the dignity of the Brazilian Negro as well as the integrity of his cultural heritage. We do not have the apartheid laws of South Africa nor the blood-tinged race relations of the United States. Nevertheless, a more subtle mechanism has grown up in the country, a kind of "white lynching," bloodless, of the physical body of the Negro by means of the glorified miscegenation. Because of the cult of miscegenation, the assimilative and acculturative process made the integral existence of the Negro impossible as far as spirit and culture are concerned. The so-called Afonso Arinos Law (1950) punishes racial discrimination, but it is powerless in the face of the crime of color prejudice that is shown, for example, in the truly morbid anxiety for the acquisition of the status of "whiteness." The Negro sociologist Guerreiro Ramos emphasized this anxiety in a study that was both rigorously scientific and ironical, *Patologia Social do "Branco" Brasileiro* (The Social Pathology of the Brazilian "White"), 1955.

There are more than enough reasons that justify the aims of TEN to go beyond the repetitive primitiveness inherent in the folklore, the skits, and the popular entertainments left over from the period of slavery that have been mentioned above. To reproduce them would simply mean an unpardonable retreat to the formerly unsuccessful attempts to slow down the flow of life and to retard the socio-historical process in whose bosom, both as *objects* and *subjects* — agents and those acted upon — we were participating in a common effort to free the Afro-Brazilian masses from their inferior condition as regards culture and social status. Skits and folklore were not the only things lacking in pretended quality. The so-called erudite theater was also completely lacking, and the only texts worthy of mention were those in the short sketch made previously. We were forced to have recourse to another play by Eugene O'Neill, *All God's Chillun Got Wings*. The actors, Ruth de Sousa, Ilena Teixeira, Jose Medeiros, Abdias do Nascimento, the director Aguinaldo Camargo, and the sets designer Mario de Murtas, were the main ones responsible for its presentation in 1946 in the Teatro Fenix. The critic for *O Jornal* pointed out that the leading actors "Abdias do Nascimento and Ilena Teixeira revealed a certain capacity for tragedy," while Cristiano Machado in *Vanguarda* said:

> The first [Abdias do Nascimento], who is certainly one of the most powerful and outstanding figures that Negro art has produced in Brazil, knew how to fill the role. . . . It is not enough to put on O'Neill; the author of *All God's Chillun Got Wings* demands that one knows how to put the play on. That was what happened during the performance we attended at the *Fenix*.

In the following year, 1947, we finally had the first Brazilian work written expressly for TEN — *O Filho Prodigo* (The Prodigal Son). Lucio Cardoso, the author, took the inspiration for his drama in verse from the Bible: a Negro family lost in the desert. Except for the father, who as a young man had walked many days and many nights to see the sea, no one had ever seen a white person. Assur is the most curious of the children. One night they take a *peregrina* (pilgrim) into their home. When she takes off the mysterious black veils that cover her face, there is revealed a white woman with a moon-like light. The *peregrina* seduces young Assur, who leaves with her for the unknown world. With sets by Santa Rosa — the mulatto who revolutionized Brazilian scenic art — and main roles by Aguinaldo Camargo, Ruth de Sousa, Jose Maria Monteiro, Abdias do Nascimento, Haroldo Costa, and Roney da Silva, *O Filho Prodigo* was considered by some critics to be the best play of the season.

Immediately following *O Filho Prodigo*, TEN produced another play written for it by Joaquim Ribeiro, *Aruanda*. Working with folkloric themes from Bahia, the author in a rough way shows the psychological ambivalence of a half-breed girl and how the Negro gods live with mortals. Rosa Mulata, culturally assimilated, does not believe in the *orixas*, the Negro gods. One night, her husband, Quele, a *filho-de-santo*, a kind of acolyte, upon returning from the *terreiro*, the African "chapel," sings a *ponto* from the *candomble* ceremony. The song invokes Gangazuma, who comes from Aruanda and possesses the body of Quele; and through her own husband, possessed by the god, Rosa Mulata becomes an adulteress. She and Gangazuma become lovers. A *cavalo* (horse) or *aparelho* (machine), unaware, Quele does not know what he is doing while he is *atuado* (possessed). As husband, however, he senses the coolness of his wife. Rosa now rejects him during the usual periods of love. Quele becomes desperate with jealousy. Rosa Mulata never goes out, and no one ever visits their poor home. With whom is she deceiving him? He spies on his wife until he surprises her in the act of confessing to her old mother. Now he knows everything. How can he avenge himself on his rival, an *orixa*, a spirit? Since the only possible course would be to punish his unfaithful wife, he thinks about killing her. But he reflects and decides against it. Death would not be a punishment but a prize. Dead, Rosa would be able to go more quickly to the arms of her lover in the enchanted realm of Aruanda. The gods do not like ugly women, and the recourse would be to disfigure her. By destroying her beauty he would automatically kill Gangazuma's love.

Our production was a completely unified show, dancing, music, mime, dramatic poetry, all harmonized and coherent. We used music by Gentil Puget and authentic *pontos* taken from *terreiros*.

The results brought forth this comment by the poet Tasso da Silveira: "It is a curious mixture of tragedy, operetta, and ballet. The script is actually a simple sketch: a few schematic situations, some short dialogs, and the rest is music, dancing, and song. What comes out of all of this is a magnificent presentation of primitive poetry."

Outstanding among the actors was Claudiano Filho in the role of Pai Joao. When the run was over, the dozens of drummers, singers, and dancers organized another group; after using various names, it became famous as the Brasiliana, playing all over Europe for ten years.

There is one author who divides the Brazilian theater into two phases, the ancient and the modern. Nelson Rodrigues is the author of *Anjo Negro* (Black Angel), a play whose tragic language reaches the theater's highest level. He bases his plot on the marriage of a Negro with a white woman. Ismael and Virginia stand out like two hermetic and implacable islands in their hatred. Color produces a hypersensitivity that brings on the dramatic action and reduces the couple to the state of unreconcilable enemies. Virginia kills the black offspring; Ismael blinds his white daughter. It is the biblical law of a tooth for a tooth played out in a life for a life and a crime for a crime. They are monsters bred by racism, which in this play has its most beautiful and terrible condemnation. When the aunt warns Ismael about his wife: "She betrayed you in order to have a white child," Ismael answers: "I have always hated being black." The prisoner of the walls built up by her husband to keep her away from the desire of other men, Virginia threatens: "I understood that a white child would come to avenge me. Against you, to avenge me against you and all Negroes." Unfortunately, the production of *Anjo Negro* (1948) did not measure up to the creative authenticity of Nelson Rodrigues. The director, Ziembinski, adopted the criterion of over-playing the aesthetic parts of the play, to the detriment of the racial content, and authorized the condemnable practice of making up a white actor in blackface to play the role of Ismael. (The producer Maria Della Costa would do the same thing when she put on *Gimba*, by Camargo Guarnieri, in which she herself wore dark make-up to play the leading role of a mulatto woman from the hillside slums.)

Anjo Negro had a great deal of trouble with the censors. Several difficulties were revealed to us by Nelson Rodrigues. When the play was selected to be part of the repertory of the official season of the Teatro Municipal in Rio de Janeiro, the authorities imposed one condition: that the main role of *Anjo Negro* be played by a white actor in blackface. They were afraid that after the performance and in the company of other Negroes, the one who played Ismael would go out on the streets in search of white women to rape. It sounds like a funny story, but there was no irony or humor in it. The fact is, moreover, that the same condition for similar reasons was repeated in 1957, in the staging of *Pedro Mico* (Pedro the Monkey) by Antonio Callado. The press reflected the apprehension of certain classes that the slum population might interpret the play as an invitation to direct action. The inhabitants of the *favelas* (Negro in the majority) would come down from the hills and commit aggression a la Pedro Mico, who wanted to repeat the deeds of the Zumbi (prince) of Palmares (republic organized by runaway slaves). Antonio Callado had written a work of major importance, sacrificed in its production by the Teatro Nacional de Comedia (Ministry of Education and Culture) by the caricaturesque figure of Pedro Mico in stove-black.

Jose de Morais Pinho wrote *Filhos de Santo,* set in his native Recife. It intertwines questions of mysticism and exploitation of *Xango* ceremony (the Pernambucan variety of the Bahian *candomble*) with the police persecution of striking workers. It is concerned with the morbid love of a white man for a Negro girl, Lindalva, who develops tuberculosis from her hard work in a factory. Serious, well-constructed, *Filhos de Santo* was presented in the Teatro Regina (Rio de Janeiro, 1949). Pai Roque speaks to Lourenco about his sister's illness, and the striking worker replies: "The work of the white bosses. Damn them. Someday I want to see those swine standing on their feet and working for the people." The *pai-de-santo* Roque replies as a person of experience: "It will be very difficult, my son. Only if every Negro thought like you, like me. . . . But so many of them, all they have to do is see a white face for them to lower their heads right away like capons. . . ." But the fact is that Lourenco is young, does not lose heart, and he says that he could always find enough Negroes who were ready, and that was why he still had hope: "It's a matter of having the power. Faith in the saints and confidence in their comrades, that's what the people have a lot of. What they don't have is power." We might say that the aims set forth by Lourenco are being attained with the liberation of almost all Africa. And also — why not say so? — the ferment among Negroes in the United States. To paraphrase Toynbee, in view of certain historical conditions, a decisive role is reserved for the American Negro in a new direction — political and cultural — for colored people the world over. It would be, in a manner of speaking, the harvest of the heritage passed on by the present generation of great Negroes— Leopold Sedar Senghor, Kwame Nkrumah, the late Langston Hughes, Jomo Kenyatta, Aime Cesaire, Sekou Toure, Nicolas Guillen, Peter Abrahams, Alioune Diop, the late Patrice Lumumba, James Baldwin, Mario de Andrade. The world has only just begun to be viewed by the Negro and Africa; mankind has just begun to perceive the unexpected black constellation of model men.

The Medea legend suggested to Agostinho Olavo his work *Alem do Rio* (Beyond the River), 1957. The author took only the backbone of the Greek tale and from it produced an original play. He tells the story of an African queen who was sold into slavery and brought to Brazil in the seventeenth century. Made the mistress of the white master, she betrays her people, is despised by her former subjects, now slaves, and becomes an abandoned and lonely queen except for the love of Jasao and her two white children. The day comes when her lover wants a home, a normal marriage like other slave-owners — that is, a white wife, social position. Jasao breaks off with Medea, but he wants to take his children with him. The queen drowns her children in the river, returns to her people and says to them: "Voices, oh, voices of my race, oh, voices, where are you? Why are you silent now? The black woman has cast off the white man. Medea spits out that name and Jinga comes back to her race to reign again." The dynamics of the play are based on folkloric songs and dances of the Negroes — *maracatu, candomble* — and on the cries of peddlers of flowers, fruits, and songbirds.

We believe *Alem do Rio* would have had a dramatic impact on the First World Festival of Negro Arts in Dakar last year, where TEN had planned to present it. In summing up the episode of racial intolerance on the part of our Foreign Ministry — leaving TEN out of our delegation — we wrote an open letter to the members of the Festival, to UNESCO, and to the government of the Republic of Senegal. For the most spurious reasons, TEN was excluded, and *Alem do Rio* still awaits an opportunity to be played.

Romeu Crusoe, a Negro from the Northeast, translated his experiences in life into the play *O Castigo de Axala* (The Punishment of Oxala), 1961, produced by an amateur group. Os Peregrinos, in the Teatro da Escola Martins Pena in Rio de Janeiro. In 1951, Abrias do Nascimento wrote the Negro mystery *Sortilegio*, whose production was forbidden by the censors. For many years the author tried to free the play from its censorship, condemned, among other grounds, on that of immorality. Finally, in 1957, TEN presented *Sortilegio* at the Teatro Municipal (in Rio de Janeiro and in Sao Paulo), directed by Leo Jusi, sets by Enrico Bianco, and music by Abigail Moura, conductor of the Afro-Brazilian Orchestra. The *mystery* had its vital nerve in the culture shock, and it proposed a Negro aesthetic as an essential part of the make-up of a genuinely Brazilian play. After speaking about the dance of the *Orixas* and the Dead, the songs of the acolyte *filhas-de-santo*, the realism of the racial question mixed in with the poetry of the *macumba* of Rio de Janeiro, Professor Roger Bastide of the Sorbonne added, speaking about *Sortilegio*:

> It was a great pleasure for me to read this play — the first manifestation of a Negro theater written by a Brazilian of color, something I have wanted for a long time. There are two ways in which one can judge the play: either from the point of view of ideas, or from the point of view of theater. From the point of view of ideas, it is the drama of the Negro, a marginal person between two cultures, the Latin and the African (the same as between two women, unfortunately both prostitutes); one can argue with the solution, the return to Africa. . . . The salvation is in the mechanics tied to an African mystique, and Brazil can bring this message of cultural brotherhood to the world. But from the point of view of theater, this return to Africa is pathetic; by means of the drink of Exu and madness, a whole world returning to the darkness of its soul. . . .

When he saw the play, Guerreiro Ramos thought: "Anyone who is not completely perverted by the Aryan aesthetic models should certainly be sensitive to what is new and revolutionary in this play." Nelson Rodrigues added: "In its strong and harmonious dramatic structure, in its vigorous poetry, in its uninterrupted drama, it makes up a great aesthetic experience for the viewer." Some critics, both black and white, took up the age-old suspicion of the personalization of the Negro and accused the author of trying for a new racism: black racism.

Except for *Pedro Mico* and *Gimba*, the last nine works mentioned above were put together in a book published by TEN in 1961 — *Dramas para Negroes e Prologo para Brancos* (Dramas for Negroes and a Prologue for Whites) — which is the first anthology of the Negro theater. The documents referring to various aspects of the movement — critical pieces, chronicles, short essays, etc. — make up the book entitled *Teatro Experimental do Negro — Testemunhas* (Experimental Theater of the Negro — Testimony), 1966. The bibliography of the Negro theater is still in the making. Among plays waiting for production we can mention a few: *Oxum Abalo, Iansan, Mulher de Xango* (Iansan, Wife of Xango), and *A Orelha de Oba* (The Ear of Oba), all by Zora Seljan. They are Afro-Brazilian myths recreated in their purity and worthy of their origin. Besides the seriousness of her research, the works of Zora Seljan are a part, in a sensitive and beautiful way, of this humanistic moment of the rise of African culture in the world. These plays were published by GRD in 1958, *Tres Mulheres de Xango* (Three Wives of Xango).

For the decade between 1950 and 1960 there are: *Orfeu Negro* (Black Orpheus), by Ironides Rodrigues; *O Processo do Cristo Negro* (The Trial of the Black Christ), by Ariano Saussuna; *Um Caso de Kele* (A Case of Kele), by Fernando Campos; *Caim e Abel* (Cain and Abel), by Eva Ban; and *O Cavalo e o Santo* (The Horse and the Saint), *Laio se Matou* (Laio Killed Himself), and *O Logro* (The Attainment), by Augusto Boal. An enormous impression was made on critics and public when the Teatro Municipal in Rio de Janeiro presented the musical work of Vinicius de Morais, *Orfeu da Conceicao,* in 1956. Actors from TEN worked in the production put on by the author himself, directed by Leo Jusi with sets by Oscar Niemeyer. The musical is a superficial and rosy-colored picture of life in the Rio hillside slums, with beautiful sambas by Vinicius and Antonio Carlos Jobim, and without any great consequences or meaning from the point of view of authenticity.

As would be natural and expected, the birth of TEN stirred up the Negro. Following its example, or even to oppose it, other groups appeared. Negroes in Sao Paulo also formed a Teatro Experimental do Negro, which has presented in its repertory, among other works, *The Mulatto,* by Langston Hughes. Hughes, like O'Neill, gave permission for TEN to put on his play, which had Aurea Campos in the role of Cora, the tragic mother of the lynched mulatto. A different group in Sao Paulo presented recently (1966) *Blues for Mr. Charlie,* by James Baldwin. There have been other movements, still not off the ground, by Negroes in Porto Alegre, Belo Horizonte, and Salvador.

In Rio de Janeiro, since the 1950s, there has been in existence the Teatro Popular Brasileiro (Brazilian Popular Theater), organized by the Negro poet Solano Trindade, with the exclusive aim of putting on stage Brazilian folklore in its purity and integrity. Its cast is for the most part made up of Negro actors, and the TPB has already traveled to Europe and plays quite often in Sao Paulo.

Another group in Rio de Janeiro, founded last year, is the Grupo de Acao (Action Group), under the leadership of Milton Goncalves. It opened with *Memorias de um Sargento de Milicias* (Memoirs of a Militia Sergeant), adapted by Milor Fernandes from the novel of the same name by Manuel Antonio de Almeida (1852). At the present time, the Grupo has on the boards *Arena Conta Zumbi* (Arena Tells About Zumbi), by Augusto Boal and Camargo Guarnieri, a musical originally presented by the Teatro de Arena (Rio de Janeiro and Sao Paulo) with an all-white cast. "It was what befit the race of black men: the *Befindlichkeit* of freedom," the poet Gerardo Melo Mourao said. The locale of the musical is the most famous redoubt of antislavery feeling in colonial Brazil, the Republic of Palmares.

We have already spoken of the Braziliana group, which right now is leaving for a new tour in Europe with its repertory of rhythms, dances, music, and songs of folkloric origin. In this field, mention should be made of the ballerina Mercedes Batista. At the instance of TEN, Katherine Dunham awarded her a fellowship at her school in New York, where Mercedes Batista spent a year. When she returned to Brazil, TEN made her the choreographer and first ballerina of our production *Rapsodia Negra* (Negro Rhapsody), 1952, in which Lea Garcia showed herself to be an exceptionally talented actress, *Rapsodia Negra* served as a fulcrum and steppingstone for Mercedes Batista to go on to create her own school of the dance and her Ballet Folclorico Mercedes Batista.

On a certain occasion when I was describing TEN, I had the opportunity to emphasize that

> it is a field of psychological polarization where the nucleus of a social movement of great proportions is forming. The great masses of colored people, of a cultural and educational level that is usually low due to socio-historical conditions, has never become organized on the basis of abstract programs. The Negro people have always organized themselves on objective grounds, albeit under the effect of religious appeals or recreational interests. The *terreiros* and *samba* schools are Negro institutions of great vitality and with profound roots, one might say, in virtue of their earthy origins. What we should grasp from this fact is the idea that we will only be able to bring the colored masses together by means of the manipulation of paideumatic survivals . . . in society and that are still connected to their African cultural roots. It is not with easy-chair thinking that we will attain and organize this mass, but by capturing and sublimating their deeply ingenuous existence, which calls for the joining together of a certain morphological intuition with sociological sense. With

these words I wish to make clear that TEN is not a political society, nor is it simply an artistic gathering, but a socio-racial experiment, having as its aim the gradual attainment by the Negro people — with admittance only into the peasant and working classes — of the manners of behavior of the middle and upper classes of Brazilian society.

We always try to emphasize a norm of action that will be neither idealistic nor ideological, because we desire the transformation of an adverse reality without recourse to truculence, without the radicalization of hate.

Certain parallel movements can be noted, such as the Group Therapy Seminar under the direction of Professor Guerreiro Ramos, which has as its function the study and therapy of the emotional tensions of the Negro; contests such as that of Rainha das Mulatas (Queen of Mulattoes) and Boneca de Pixe, both pedagogical instruments that attempt to define a type of beauty in the Afro-Brazilian woman, and the subsequent education of public taste, so perverted by the pressure and exclusive celebration of white models of beauty. Even a contest in the plastic arts entitled Cristo Negro (Black Christ), 1955, had similar ends.

Under the patronage of TEN, two sessions were held of the Convencao Nacional do Negro (National Negro Convention), Sao Paulo, 1945, and Rio de Janeiro, 1946; the Conferencia Nacional do Negro (National Negro Conference), 1949, forerunner of the Primeiro Congresso do Negro Brasileiro (First Congress of the Brazilian Negro), 1950, and the Semana do Negro (Negro Week), 1955. Abdias do Nascimento put the results of these meetings into a book, *Estrategia do Negro Brasileiro* (Strategy of the Brazilian Negro), which the publishing firm GRD will shortly bring out.

In the year 1968, the Brazilian Negro completed eighty years of legal freedom. The Negro theater especially is still in its infancy, with many problems still awaiting solutions. An urgent necessity, for example, is a theater of its own, where it could present works and carry on cultural activities. The cessation of publication of *Quilombo,* the organ of TEN, is also a grave problem. Another problem is that of reaching the colored masses and making a permanent audience out of them. Their acquisitive powers are practically nil, and the cost of a theater ticket is relatively high. We have tried in vain to interest the National Theater service (Ministry of Education and Culture) in the project of a living theater. TEN at this moment is organizing a museum of Negro art. The exhibits will be from the work of Negro artists and from artists of other colors inspired by Negro culture or showing some aspect of Negro culture or its influence in the world. And since Negro art is not solitary, but exists in permanent interaction with other artistic manifestations, the museum of Negro art will collect, regardless of racial or national origin, the works — painting, sculpture, design, engraving, and any other form — of art that are deemed to have artistic significance.

The Experimental Theater of the Negro is a process. Negritude is a process. What is projected is an adventure in the Afro-Brazilian theater and in Negro life in Brazil. So long as the Negro does not awake completely from the torpor in which he has been wrapped, the Negro theater in Brazil will still not have said everything that it has meant to say.

ABOUT THE CONTRIBUTORS

Alvin Aubert is professor of English at the State University College at Fredonia, New York.

Lloyd W. Brown is professor of English at the University of Southern California.

Joseph Bruchac teaches English at Skidmore College, Saratoga Springs, New York.

Abdias do Nascimento is visiting professor at the State University of New York at Buffalo.

Jacob U. Gordon is director of African Studies at the University of Kansas, Lawrence, Kansas.

R. M. Lacovia is visiting assistant professor at the State University of New York at Buffalo.

John Lindberg is associate professor of English at Shippensburg (Pa.) State College.

S. Okechukwu Mezu, associate professor of French, is director of African Studies at the State University of New York at Buffalo.

Pol Ndu is lecturer in English at the University of Nigeria, Nsukka, Nigeria.

Charles E. Nnolim teaches black literature at Babson College, Babson Park, Massachusetts.

Elliott M. Schrero is professor of English at Rider College, Trenton, New Jersey.

Paul C. Sherr is professor of English at Rider College, Trenton, New Jersey.

Harold A. Waters is professor of French at the University of Rhode Island, Kingston, Rhode Island.